THE GLOBAL SHAKESPEARE SERIES

The Tragedy of MACBETH

with Related Readings

SERIES EDITORS

Dom Saliani Chris Ferguson Dr. Tim Scott

I(T)P *International Thomson Publishing*

Albany • Bonn • Boston • Cincinnati • Detroit • London • Madrid • Melbourne • Mexico City • New York • Pacific Grove • Paris • San Francisco • Singapore • Tokyo • Toronto • Washington

International Thomson Publishing, 1997

Published simultaneously in 1997 by International Thomson Limited:

ITP Nelson Canada **South-Western Educational Publishing (U.S.A.)**
Nelson ITP (Australia) **Thomas Nelson United Kingdom**

ISBN 0-17-605789-7

Cataloguing in Publication Data

Shakespeare, William, 1564-1616
Macbeth with related readings

(The global Shakespeare series)
ISBN 0-17-605789-7

1. Shakespeare, William, 1564-1616. Macbeth.
I. Saliani, Dom. II. Title. III. Series.

PR2823.A2S24 1996 822.3'3 C96-990042-2

Project Managers: Tara Steele (Canada)
Jackie Tidey (Australia)
Laurie Wendell (U.S.A.)
Series Designer: Liz Harasymczuk
Cover Illustrator: Yuan Lee
Production Editors: Sandra Manley, Kathleen ffolliott, Marcia Miron, Karen Alliston
Composition Analyst: Daryn Dewalt
Production Coordinator: Donna Brown
Permissions: Vicki Gould
Research: Lisa Brant

Printed and bound in Canada

Visit us on our website:
http://www.thomson.com

3 4 5 ML 00 99

Contents

Features of the *Global Shakespeare Series*

Introduction to the Play: Information on the date, sources, themes, and appeal of the play, notes on Shakespeare's use of verse and prose, and common stage directions all help to set a context for the play.

The Text: The *Global Shakespeare Series* is faithful to Shakespeare's full original texts. Spelling and punctuation have been modernized to make the plays accessible to today's readers. For the last 200 years, many editors have chosen to arrange and rearrange Shakespeare's words to create a consistent iambic pentameter in the text. For example, a dialogue involving short speeches would look like this:

MACBETH: Your children shall be kings.
BANQUO: You shall be King.

Together the two lines make up 10 syllables. In some cases, editors have even taken words from one line and combined them with words from another line to create the iambic pentameter pattern. Shakespeare did not do this in his original text. The *Global Shakespeare Series* has not adopted this convention. What you see is what Shakespeare wrote.

Dramatis Personae: The list of characters is organized by families or by loyalty affiliations.

Scene Summaries: Brief synopses help you to follow and anticipate developments in the plot.

Artwork and Graphics: Original artwork has been created and designed for this series by internationally acclaimed artists.

Marginal Notes: Generous notes define difficult or archaic vocabulary. In some cases, entire sentences of Shakespeare are paraphrased into modern idiom — these are identified with quotation marks.

Notes of Interest: Longer notes provide background information on Shakespeare's times or interesting interpretations of various speeches or characters.

Quotable Notables: Brief comments on various aspects of the play by authors, celebrities, and highly regarded literary critics and professors are included. The views do not necessarily reflect the views of the editors; they are merely springboards for discussion, debate, and reflection.

Related Reading References: These references indicate that there is a piece of literature in the latter part of the book that relates well to a specific scene or speech.

Considerations: Each Act is followed by a series of scene-specific "considerations." Some involve analysis and interpretation; others will offer opportunities to be creative and imaginative.

Related Readings: The second half of the text contains poems, short stories, short drama, and non-fiction pieces that are directly related to the play. These can be read for enjoyment or for enrichment. They emphasize the continuing relevance of Shakespeare in today's society.

The 10 Most Difficult Questions One Can Ask: These challenging questions are ideal for developing into research or independent study projects.

Introduction to *Macbeth*

Date and Sources

According to history, Macbeth's reign spanned the period between 1040 and 1057. Apparently he was a good king who passed many progressive laws. Shakespeare, however, paints quite a different portrait of Macbeth. Shakespeare's primary source for the play was a contemporary historical text known as *Holinshed's Chronicles* (1577). From *Holinshed's,* however, Shakespeare uses little more than the names of the characters and some very basic elements of plot.

The play did not appear in print until 1623. Some scholars believe that it was performed for King James in 1606, but no clear evidence to support this has been found. The play, as it has come down to us, may have involved more than one author. It is generally believed that the witches' scenes were added to the original play by Thomas Middleton.

The Appeal of Macbeth

Macbeth is one of Shakespeare's most popular tragedies. Perhaps this is because of its length. At 2107 lines, it is Shakespeare's shortest tragedy. *Hamlet,* by the way, is 3924 lines long.

Macbeth is also one of Shakespeare's most violent tragedies. There are over 100 references to bloodshed in this play, and the number of dead bodies that are carried off the stage is truly staggering.

The Witches also add an element to the play that has contributed to its popularity. We, like the Elizabethans, continue to be intrigued by witchcraft and magic. We see in the play *Macbeth* a contemporary morality play warning us of the dangers of trafficking with "the instruments of darkness."

Shakespeare's Verse and Prose

Many students find Shakespeare difficult to read and understand. They often ask whether or not the Elizabethans really spoke the way Shakespeare's characters do. The answer is, of course, no. Shakespeare writes using a poetic form known as *blank verse.* This produces an elevated style, which would have been very different from everyday speech during the Elizabethan period.

Furthermore, the blank verse contains a rhythm pattern known as *iambic pentameter.* What this means is that most lines contain five feet (pentameter) and each foot contains an unstressed and a stressed syllable (an iamb). In other words, as Shakespeare wrote, playing in the back of his mind was a rhythm pattern that would sound like:

da DA da DA da DA da DA da DA

London's Globe Theatre in 1616, as depicted in an engraving by C.J. Visscher.

In terms of stressed and unstressed syllables, Macbeth's first line in the play would look like this:

~ / ~ / ~ / ~ / ~ /
So foul and fair a day I have not seen.

There are also approximately 150 lines of prose in this play. Prose contrasts strongly with the elevated style of blank verse. Persons of noble birth speak in verse and servants and members of the lower classes usually speak in prose. Letters and documents, scenes of comic relief, and scenes involving madness are usually written in prose.

Incarnations of Macbeth

The story of Macbeth has been translated into a variety of art forms. In 1674, Sir William Davenant (who claimed to be Shakespeare's illegitimate son) staged an operatic version of the play. David Garrick "improved" the play in 1744 by having Macbeth die on stage after delivering an eminently forgettable death speech. Eventually the play was restored to its original form and it continues to be successful to this very day.

In 1936, Orson Welles produced the first Black production of *Macbeth*. He set his *"Voodoo" Macbeth* in Haiti with voodoo priestesses in place of the witches.

A number of feature films have been based on the story of Macbeth. British director Ken Hughes gave us *Joe Macbeth* (1955), a gangster movie that follows the plot of Shakespeare's play closely. In 1957, Japanese filmmaker Akira Kurosawa released his version of the story, entitled *Throne of Blood*. In 1971, director Roman Polanski's film treatment stunned audiences with its graphic violence and bold interpretation. *Men of Respect* (1991) is another attempt at placing the story of Macbeth in a gangster setting. One highlight of this movie is the sleepwalking scene during which a flashlight is carried instead of a candle.

A modern rock opera version entitled *From a Jack to a King* hit the stage in 1992.

The Text and Stage Directions

The edition for this text is faithful to the 1623 First Folio.

Shakespeare used stage directions very sparingly in his plays. Because he was directly involved in the production of the plays, there was little need for him to record the stage directions.

A performance at the Globe Theatre.

In this edition, the stage directions that appear in italics are Shakespeare's. Directions that are included in square brackets *[ ]* are added by the editor.

The following stage directions appear frequently in Shakespeare's plays:

Above, aloft – scene played in the balcony above the stage level or from higher up in the loft

Alarum – a loud shout, a signal call to arms

Aside – spoken directly to the audience and not heard by the others on the stage

Below, beneath – speech or scene played from below the surface of the stage. The actor stands inside an open trap-door.

Exit – he/she leaves the stage

Exeunt – they leave the stage

Flourish – fanfare of trumpets; usually announces the entrance of royalty

Hautboys – musicians enter, playing wind instruments

Omnes – all; everyone

Within – words spoken off-stage in what the audience would assume is an unseen room, a corridor, or the outdoors

The Orkneys

Western Isles

Caithness

SCOTLAND

Elgin

Inverness

Forres

Cawdor

Ross

Angus

Glamis

Birnam

Colme-kill

Dunsinane

Scone

Fife

St. Colme's Inch

Lennox

North Channel

Northumberland

Cumberland

WALES

ENGLAND

The setting for ***MACBETH***

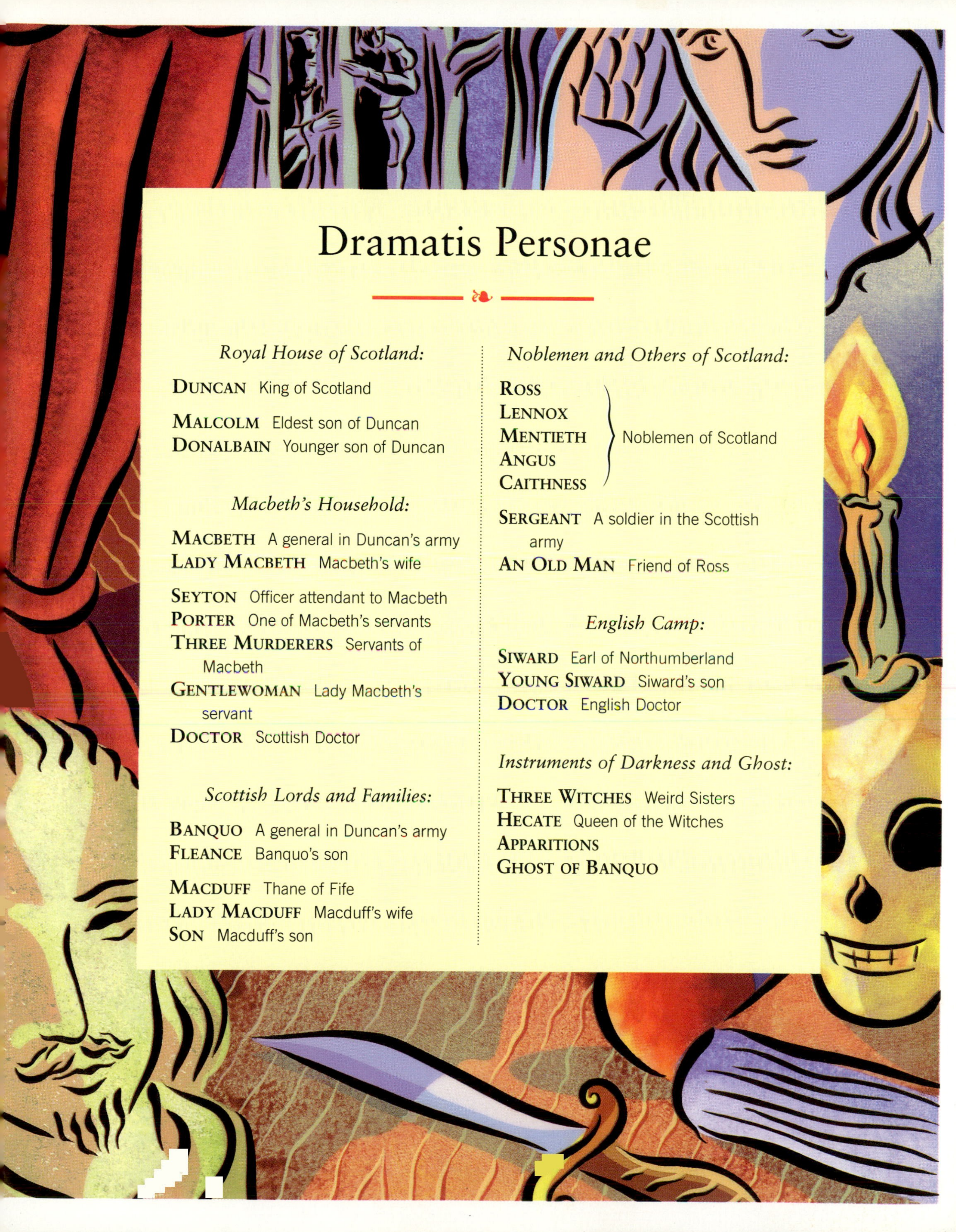

Dramatis Personae

Royal House of Scotland:

DUNCAN King of Scotland

MALCOLM Eldest son of Duncan
DONALBAIN Younger son of Duncan

Macbeth's Household:

MACBETH A general in Duncan's army
LADY MACBETH Macbeth's wife

SEYTON Officer attendant to Macbeth
PORTER One of Macbeth's servants
THREE MURDERERS Servants of Macbeth
GENTLEWOMAN Lady Macbeth's servant
DOCTOR Scottish Doctor

Scottish Lords and Families:

BANQUO A general in Duncan's army
FLEANCE Banquo's son

MACDUFF Thane of Fife
LADY MACDUFF Macduff's wife
SON Macduff's son

Noblemen and Others of Scotland:

ROSS, **LENNOX**, **MENTIETH**, **ANGUS**, **CAITHNESS** — Noblemen of Scotland

SERGEANT A soldier in the Scottish army
AN OLD MAN Friend of Ross

English Camp:

SIWARD Earl of Northumberland
YOUNG SIWARD Siward's son
DOCTOR English Doctor

Instruments of Darkness and Ghost:

THREE WITCHES Weird Sisters
HECATE Queen of the Witches
APPARITIONS
GHOST OF BANQUO

Act One

Scene 1

As a battle rages, the Weird Sisters appear and agree that they will meet with Macbeth once the battle is over.

A desert place.

Thunder and lightning. Enter three Witches.

FIRST WITCH: When shall we three meet again?
In thunder, lightning, or in rain?
SECOND WITCH: When the hurlyburly's done,
When the battle's lost and won.
THIRD WITCH: That will be ere the set of sun.
FIRST WITCH: Where the place?
SECOND WITCH: Upon the heath.
THIRD WITCH: There to meet with Macbeth.
FIRST WITCH: I come, Graymalkin.
ALL: Paddock calls anon.
Fair is foul, and foul is fair.
Hover through the fog and filthy air.

Exeunt.

3. *hurlyburly* – turmoil, confusion, fighting
5. *ere* – before

7. *heath* – barren place

9. *Graymalkin* – a common name for a grey cat
10. *Paddock* – toad
9 – 10. Toads and cats are "familiars" or demon associates of witches.

11 – 12. These lines set the tone for the play. The Weird Sisters suggest that they inhabit a world in which the moral order has been reversed, a world in which it is difficult to tell what is truly fair or good and what is indeed foul and evil. This scene introduces a recurrent theme in the play – the discrepancy between appearance and reality.

Act One

Scene 2

A camp near Forres.

Alarum within. Enter King, Malcolm, Donalbain, Lennox, with Attendants, meeting a bleeding Sergeant.

KING: What bloody man is that? He can report,
As seemeth by his plight, of the revolt
The newest state.
MALCOLM: This is the Sergeant
Who, like a good and hardy soldier fought
'Gainst my captivity. — Hail, brave friend!
Say to the King the knowledge of the broil
As thou didst leave it.
SERGEANT: Doubtful it stood,
As two spent swimmers that do cling together
And choke their art. The merciless Macdonwald
(Worthy to be a rebel, for to that
The multiplying villainies of nature
Do swarm upon him) from the Western Isles
Of kerns and gallowglasses is supplied;
And Fortune, on his damned quarrel smiling,
Showed like a rebel's whore. But all's too weak;
For brave Macbeth (well he deserves that name)
Disdaining Fortune, with his brandished steel,
Which smoked with bloody execution,
Like Valour's minion carved out his passage,
Till he faced the slave,
Which never shook hands, nor bade farewell to him,
Till he unseamed him from the nave to the chops,
And fixed his head upon our battlements.
KING: O valiant cousin! Worthy gentleman!
SERGEANT: As whence the sun begins his reflection
Shipwrecking storms and direful thunders break,

The valiant and worthy character of Macbeth is established in two reports of different battles delivered to King Duncan. The Thane of Cawdor, a traitor, has been captured. Duncan orders that the traitor be executed and that his title be given to Macbeth in recognition of his heroic efforts.

Shakespeare uses "blood" well over a hundred times in this play.

1 – 3. "judging by his physical condition, he can report the latest news of the revolt."

10. *spent* – exhausted
11. *choke their art* – drown by hanging on to each other
13. *villainies of nature* – lice
15. *kerns and gallowglasses* – light-armed foot soldiers and horsemen armed with axes
16 – 17. "Fortune seemed to be siding with the cause of the rebels."
20. *smoked* – steamed (with hot blood)
21. *minion* – darling; pet
24. "Till he ripped him open from the navel to his chin"
26. *cousin* – Macbeth and Duncan were both grandchildren of King Malcolm.

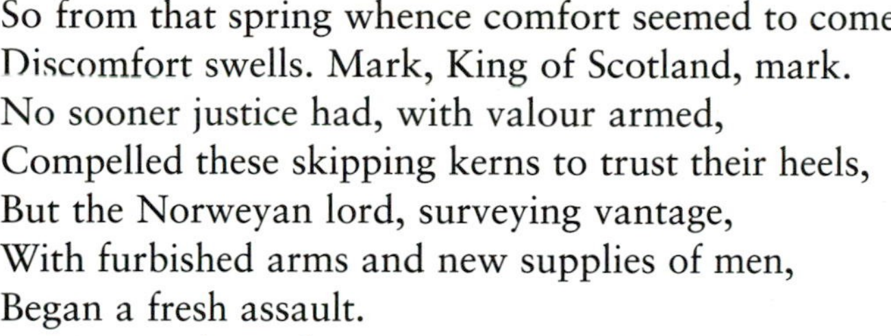

So from that spring whence comfort seemed to come
Discomfort swells. Mark, King of Scotland, mark.
No sooner justice had, with valour armed,
Compelled these skipping kerns to trust their heels,
But the Norweyan lord, surveying vantage,
With furbished arms and new supplies of men,
Began a fresh assault.

KING: Dismayed not this our captains, Macbeth and
Banquo?

SERGEANT: Yes, as sparrows eagles,
Or the hare the lion.
If I say sooth, I must report they were
As cannons overcharged with double cracks,
So they doubly redoubled strokes upon the foe.
Except they meant to bathe in reeking wounds,
Or memorize another Golgotha,
I cannot tell — but I am faint,
My gashes cry for help.

KING: So well thy words become thee as thy wounds.
They smack of honour both. Go get him surgeons.

[Exit Sergeant, attended.]

Who comes here?

Enter Ross and Angus.

MALCOLM: The worthy Thane of Ross.

LENNOX: What a haste looks through his eyes!
So should he look that seems to speak things strange.

ROSS: God save the King!

KING: Whence camest thou, worthy Thane?

ROSS: From Fife, great King,
Where the Norweyan banners flout the sky
And fan our people cold.
Norway himself, with terrible numbers,
Assisted by that most disloyal traitor
The Thane of Cawdor, began a dismal conflict,
Till that Bellona's bridegroom, lapped in proof,
Confronted him with self-comparisons,
Point against point, rebellious, arm 'gainst arm,
Curbing his lavish spirit, and, to conclude,
The victory fell on us.

KING: Great happiness!

ROSS: That now Sweno, the Norways' king,

32. *skipping kerns* – quickly retreating foot soldiers
33. *surveying vantage* – seeing an opportunity
34. *furbished* – fresh

40. *sooth* – truth
41. "As cannons double-loaded with gunpowder charges"
43. *except* – unless
44. "Or make the place memorable like Golgotha" (Golgotha was the site of Christ's crucifixion; it means "the place of skulls.")

50. *Thane* – chief of a clan; almost equivalent in rank to an earl
55. *Fife* – located in eastern Scotland. See map on page 8.
56. *flout* – insult; mock
60. *dismal* – damaging (to the Scots)
61. *Bellona* – goddess of war
61. *lapped in proof* – in full battle gear
62. *self-comparisons* – equalled him in courage and deeds
64. *lavish* – insolent; over-confident

68. "Desires to negotiate a peace"
69. *deign* – permit
70. *disbursed* – paid out
70. *Saint Colme's Inch* – island in the Firth of Forth. See map on page 8.

Craves composition.
Nor would we deign him burial of his men
Till he disbursed, at Saint Colme's Inch,
Ten thousand dollars to our general use.

KING: No more that Thane of Cawdor shall deceive - irony
Our bosom interest. Go pronounce his present death,
And with his former title greet Macbeth.

ROSS: I'll see it done.

KING: What he hath lost, noble Macbeth hath won.

Exeunt.

another battle (invasion of noweigans) fought + won by macbeth. (macbeth in two places at once)

Act One
Scene 3

The battle is done and the Weird Sisters meet again. They greet Macbeth and Banquo with a series of prophecies. They predict that Macbeth will not only be Thane of Cawdor but will also be King, and that Banquo will be father to a line of kings. Ross and Angus arrive with news that Macbeth is the new Thane of Cawdor, thus fulfilling the first of the prophecies.

A heath.

Thunder. Enter the three Witches.

FIRST WITCH: Where hast thou been, sister?
SECOND WITCH: Killing swine.
THIRD WITCH: Sister, where thou?
FIRST WITCH: A sailor's wife had chestnuts in her lap,
And munched, and munched, and munched.
"Give me," quoth I.
"Aroint thee, witch!" the rump-fed ronyon cries.
Her husband's to Aleppo gone, master of the Tiger;
But in a sieve I'll thither sail,
And, like a rat without a tail
I'll do, I'll do, and I'll do.
SECOND WITCH: I'll give thee a wind.
FIRST WITCH: Thou art kind.
THIRD WITCH: And I another.
FIRST WITCH: I myself have all the other,
And the very ports they blow,
All the quarters that they know
In the shipman's card.
I'll drain him dry as hay;
Sleep shall neither night nor day
Hang upon his penthouse lid.
He shall live a man forbid.
Weary seven-nights, nine times nine
Shall he dwindle, peak, and pine.
Though his bark cannot be lost,
Yet it shall be tempest-tossed.
Look what I have.
SECOND WITCH: Show me! Show me!
FIRST WITCH: Here I have a pilot's thumb,

7. "'Go away, you witch!' the large-bottomed hag cries."

11. *do* – bewitch

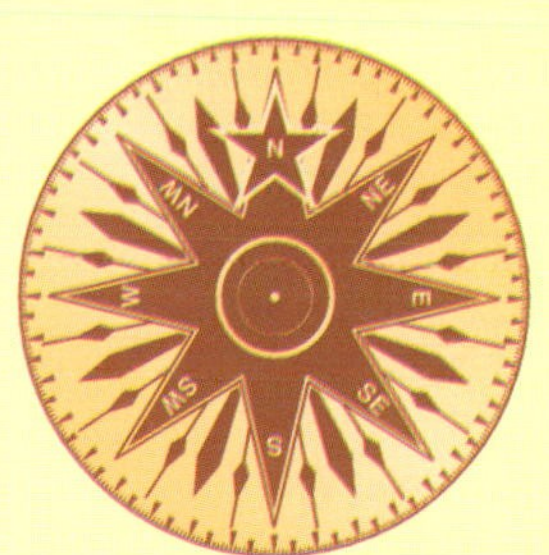

shipman's card

18. *shipman's card* – sailor's compass or chart
21. *penthouse lid* – eyelids

29. *thumb* – Parts of bodies of those who died violently were used in casting spells.

33. *Weird Sisters* – "Wyrd" is the Anglo–Saxon word for "fate." In *Holinshed's Chronicles*, the three sisters are specifically referred to as the "goddesses of destiny." This would explain why Macbeth is so quick to listen to their predictions. Such would not be the case if they were merely witches and instruments of evil.

34. *Posters* – persons who travel swiftly

39. Notice that Macbeth's first words echo the witches' final incantation in the first scene of the play.

40. *Forres* – site of the King's castle. See map on page 8.

43. *aught* – anything

45. *choppy* – chapped

Wrecked as homeward he did come.

Drum within.

THIRD WITCH: A drum, a drum!
Macbeth doth come.
ALL: The Weird Sisters, hand in hand,
Posters of the sea and land,
Thus do go about, about,
Thrice to thine, and thrice to mine,
And thrice again, to make up nine.
Peace! The charm's wound up.

Enter Macbeth and Banquo.

MACBETH: So foul and fair a day I have not seen.
BANQUO: How far is it called to Forres? What are these
So withered and so wild in their attire,
That look not like the inhabitants of the earth,
And yet are on it? Live you, or are you aught
That man may question? You seem to understand me,
By each at once her choppy finger laying
Upon her skinny lips. You should be women,
And yet your beards forbid me to interpret
That you are so.

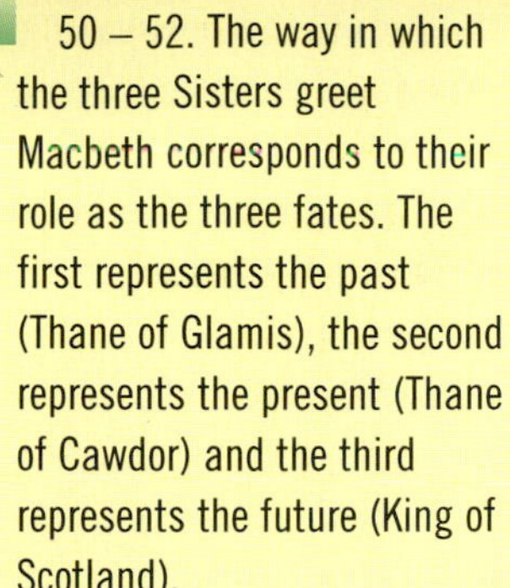

MACBETH: Speak, if you can. What are you?
FIRST WITCH: All hail, Macbeth, hail to thee, Thane
of Glamis!
SECOND WITCH: All hail, Macbeth, hail to thee, Thane
of Cawdor!
THIRD WITCH: All hail, Macbeth, that shalt be King hereafter!
BANQUO: Good sir, why do you start, and seem to fear
Things that do sound so fair? In the name of truth,
Are ye fantastical or that indeed
Which outwardly ye show? My noble partner
You greet with present grace and great prediction
Of noble having and of royal hope,
That he seems rapt withal. To me you speak not.
If you can look into the seeds of time
And say which grain will grow and which will not,
Speak then to me, who neither beg nor fear
Your favours nor your hate.
FIRST WITCH: Hail!
SECOND WITCH: Hail!
THIRD WITCH: Hail!
FIRST WITCH: Lesser than Macbeth, and greater.
SECOND WITCH: Not so happy, yet much happier.
THIRD WITCH: Thou shalt get kings, though thou be none.
So all hail, Macbeth and Banquo!
FIRST WITCH: Banquo and Macbeth, all hail!

50 – 52. The way in which the three Sisters greet Macbeth corresponds to their role as the three fates. The first represents the past (Thane of Glamis), the second represents the present (Thane of Cawdor) and the third represents the future (King of Scotland).

69. "Although you will father a line of kings, you will not be one yourself."

"The Weird Sisters present nouns rather than verbs. They put titles on Macbeth without telling what actions he must carry out to attain those titles. It is Lady Macbeth who supplies the verbs."
– Susan Snyder –
American Professor of English and critic

72. *imperfect* – because they are ambiguous and have not provided sufficient details

73. *Sinel* – Macbeth's father

78. *owe* – have received

84. *corporal* – substantial, solid

88. *insane root* – plant which causes madness, or hallucinations

97 – 98. "The King was left speechless, not knowing whether he should express amazement or praise for Macbeth's deeds in battle."

103. *post* – messenger

108. *herald* – summon

110. *earnest* – pledge, partial payment

MACBETH: Stay, you imperfect speakers, tell me more.
By Sinel's death I know I am Thane of Glamis,
But how of Cawdor? The Thane of Cawdor lives,
A prosperous gentleman, and to be King
Stands not within the prospect of belief,
No more than to be Cawdor. Say from whence
You owe this strange intelligence, or why
Upon this blasted heath you stop our way
With such prophetic greeting?
Speak, I charge you.

Witches vanish.

BANQUO: The earth hath bubbles as the water has,
And these are of them. Whither are they vanished?
MACBETH: Into the air, and what seemed corporal
Melted as breath into the wind.
Would they had stayed!
BANQUO: Were such things here as we do speak about?
Or have we eaten on the insane root
That takes the reason prisoner?
MACBETH: Your children shall be kings.
BANQUO: You shall be King.
MACBETH: And Thane of Cawdor too. Went it not so?
BANQUO: To the selfsame tune and words. Who's here?

Enter Ross and Angus.

ROSS: The King hath happily received, Macbeth,
The news of thy success, and when he reads
Thy personal venture in the rebels' fight,
His wonders and his praises do contend
Which should be thine or his. Silenced with that,
In viewing over the rest of the selfsame day,
He finds thee in the stout Norweyan ranks,
Nothing afeard of what thyself didst make,
Strange images of death. As thick as hail
Came post with post, and every one did bear
Thy praises in his kingdom's great defense,
And poured them down before him.
ANGUS: We are sent
To give thee, from our royal master, thanks,
Only to herald thee into his sight,
Not pay thee.
ROSS: And for an earnest of a greater honour,

He bade me, from him, call thee Thane of Cawdor.
In which addition, hail, most worthy Thane,
For it is thine.

Banquo: What, can the devil speak true?

Macbeth: The Thane of Cawdor lives.
Why do you dress me in borrowed robes?

Angus: Who was the Thane lives yet,
But under heavy judgement bears that life
Which he deserves to lose.
Whether he was combined with those of Norway,
Or did line the rebel with hidden help
And vantage, or that with both he laboured
In his country's wreck, I know not,
But treasons capital, confessed and proved,
Have overthrown him.

Macbeth: *[Aside.]* Glamis, and Thane of Cawdor!
The greatest is behind. *[To Ross and Angus.]* Thanks
for your pains.
[Aside to Banquo.]
Do you not hope your children shall be kings,
When those that gave the Thane of Cawdor to me
Promised no less to them?

Banquo: *[Aside to Macbeth.]* That, trusted home,
Might yet enkindle you unto the crown,
Besides the Thane of Cawdor. But 'tis strange,
And oftentimes, to win us to our harm,
The instruments of darkness tell us truths,
Win us with honest trifles, to betray us
In deepest consequence —
Cousins, a word, I pray you.

Macbeth: *[Aside.]* Two truths are told,
As happy prologues to the swelling act
Of the imperial theme — I thank you, gentlemen.
[Aside.] This supernatural soliciting
Cannot be ill, cannot be good.
If ill, why hath it given me earnest of success,
Commencing in a truth? I am Thane of Cawdor.
If good, why do I yield to that suggestion
Whose horrid image doth unfix my hair
And make my seated heart knock at my ribs,
Against the use of nature? Present fears
Are less than horrible imaginings.
My thought, whose murder yet is but fantastical,
Shakes so my single state of man
That function is smothered in surmise

112. *addition* – title

118. *heavy judgement* – sentence of death

120. *combined* – secretly allied; in league with

121. *line* – provide

124. *capital* – punishable by death

131. *trusted home* – believed completely

132. *enkindle* – fire; raise your hopes

134. "And often, to succeed in bringing about our destruction"

137. *deepest consequence* – of utmost importance

142. *soliciting* – prompting; promises of prosperity

147. *unfix my hair* – make my hair stand on end

149 – 150. "Present objects of fear are not as terrifying as those that we imagine."

151. "My mind, which merely contains the thought of murder"

152. *single state* – harmonious working

153. *surmise* – thinking, conjecturing

And nothing is, but what is not.
Banquo: Look, how our partner's rapt.
Macbeth: *[Aside.]* If chance will have me King
Why, chance may crown me
Without my stir.
Banquo: New honours come upon him,
Like our strange garments, cleave not to their mould
But with the aid of use.
Macbeth: *[Aside.]* Come what come may,
Time and the hour runs through the roughest day.
Banquo: Worthy Macbeth, we stay upon your leisure.
Macbeth: Give me your favour.
My dull brain was wrought with things forgotten.
Kind gentlemen, your pains are registered
Where every day I turn the leaf
To read them.
Let us toward the King. *[To Banquo]* Think upon
What hath chanced, and at more time,
The interim having weighed it, let us speak
Our free hearts each to other.
Banquo: Very gladly.
Macbeth: Till then, enough. —
Come, friends.

Exeunt.

154. "Nothing in the present seems as real as what my mind imagines about the future."
158. "Without my having to do anything."

163. "Time passes and even the roughest day must come to an end."
164. *stay* – wait
165. *favour* – pardon

172. *interim ... it* – "In the meantime, having thought about it"

RELATED READING

The Imagery of Macbeth – literary essay by Caroline Spurgeon (page 123)

Act One

Scene 4

Duncan hears how nobly the traitor Cawdor died. Macbeth and Banquo arrive and are warmly greeted by the gracious King. Duncan proclaims his son Malcolm heir to the throne and announces his intention to visit Macbeth's castle. Macbeth leaves to prepare for the King's arrival. Macbeth now appears resolved to act to hasten the fulfillment of the Weird Sisters' prophecies.

Forres.

The palace.

Flourish. Enter King, Lennox, Malcolm, Donalbain, and Attendants.

King: Is execution done on Cawdor?
Are not those in commission yet returned?
Malcolm: My liege, they are not yet come back.
But I have spoke with one that saw him die,
Who did report that very frankly he
Confessed his treasons, implored your Highness' pardon,
And set forth a deep repentance.
Nothing in his life became him
Like the leaving it. He died
As one that had been studied in his death
To throw away the dearest thing he owed
As 'twere a careless trifle.
King: There's no art
To find the mind's construction in the face:
He was a gentleman on whom I built
An absolute trust.

Enter Macbeth, Banquo, Ross, and Angus.

O worthiest cousin!
The sin of my ingratitude even now
Was heavy on me. Thou art so far before,
That swiftest wing of recompense is slow
To overtake thee. Would thou hadst less deserved,
That the proportion both of thanks and payment
Might have been mine! Only I have left to say,
More is thy due than more than all can pay.

2. *in commission* – those delegated to carry out the order

8. *became* – gave him dignity

11. *owed* – owned

14. *construction* – inner, true workings

19. *before* – ahead
20. *recompense* – reward
21 – 24. "I can't thank you enough."

MACBETH: The service and the loyalty I owe,
In doing it, pays itself.
Your Highness' part is to receive our duties,
And our duties are to your throne and state,
Children and servants, which do but what they should
By doing everything safe toward your love
And honour.

KING: Welcome hither.
I have begun to plant thee, and will labour
To make thee full of growing. Noble Banquo,
That hast no less deserved, nor must be known
No less to have done so. Let me infold thee
And hold thee to my heart.

BANQUO: There if I grow,
The harvest is your own.

KING: My plenteous joys,
Wanton in fullness, seek to hide themselves
In drops of sorrow. Sons, kinsmen, thanes,
And you whose places are the nearest, know
We will establish our estate upon
Our eldest, Malcolm, whom we name hereafter
The Prince of Cumberland, which honour must
Not unaccompanied invest him only,
But signs of nobleness, like stars, shall shine
On all deservers. From hence to Inverness,
And bind us further to you.

MACBETH: The rest is labour, which is not used for you.
I'll be myself the harbinger, and make joyful
The hearing of my wife with your approach.
So humbly take my leave.

KING: My worthy Cawdor!

MACBETH: *[Aside.]* The Prince of Cumberland! That is a step
On which I must fall down, or else overleap,
For in my way it lies. Stars, hide your fires!
Let not light see my black and deep desires.
The eye wink at the hand, yet let that be
Which the eye fears, when it is done, to see.

Exit.

KING: True, worthy Banquo! He is full so valiant,
And in his commendations I am fed.
It is a banquet to me. Let's after him,
Whose care is gone before to bid us welcome.
It is a peerless kinsman.

Flourish. Exeunt.

30. *safe toward* – to safeguard

36. *infold* – embrace

41. *wanton* – unrestrained

46. *Prince of Cumberland* – title given to the heir to the throne of Scotland

47. *invest* – be conferred upon

49. *Inverness* – site of Macbeth's castle. See map on page 8.

52. *harbinger* – forerunner; one who goes before to arrange lodgings

60 – 61. "Let the eye not see what the hand does, and yet let that deed be done that the eye will be afraid to look at once it is done."

63. *commendations* – praises

66. *peerless* – without equal

Act One

Scene 5

Lady Macbeth reads a letter from her husband detailing the encounter with the witches. She immediately resolves to have Duncan killed to fulfill the prophecy. A messenger brings news of the King's imminent arrival. Macbeth appears and they begin to plot the assassination of the King.

Inverness.

Macbeth's castle.

Enter Macbeth's Wife alone with a letter.

LADY MACBETH: *"They met me in the day of success, and I have learned by the perfectest report, they have more in them than mortal knowledge. When I burned in desire to question them further, they made themselves air, into which they vanished. Whiles I stood rapt in the wonder of it, came missives from the King, who all-hailed me 'Thane of Cawdor,' by which title, before, these weyward sisters saluted me and referred me to the coming on of time with 'Hail, King that shalt be!' This have I thought good to deliver thee, my dearest partner of greatness, that thou mightst not lose the dues of rejoicing by being ignorant of what greatness is promised thee. Lay it to thy heart, and farewell."*

Glamis thou art, and Cawdor, and shalt be
What thou art promised. Yet do I fear thy nature.
It is too full of the milk of human kindness
To catch the nearest way. Thou wouldst be great,
Art not without ambition, but without
The illness should attend it. What thou wouldst highly,
That wouldst thou holily; wouldst not play false,
And yet wouldst wrongly win.
Thou'dst have, great Glamis, that which cries,
Thus thou must do, if thou have it;
And that which rather thou dost fear to do
Than wishest should be undone. Hie thee hither,
That I may pour my spirits in thine ear,
And chastise with the valour of my tongue

3. *mortal* – available to mortals

10. *dues* – share

16. *wouldst* – would like very much

18. *illness ... it* – without exercising the ruthlessness that accompanies it (ambition)

26. *chastise* – drive away

27. *round* – crown
28. *metaphysical* – supernatural

"To bite at the apple is a fearful thing ... Macbeth has a wife whom the chronicle calls Gruoch. This Eve tempts this Adam. Once Macbeth has taken the first bite, he is lost. The first thing that Adam produced with Eve is Cain; the first thing that Macbeth accomplishes with Gruoch is Murder."
– Victor Hugo (1802 – 1885) French novelist, author of *Les Miserables*

44. *mortal* – murderous
44. *unsex me here* – remove from me any feminine sensitivities
48 – 50. "Let no natural stirrings of conscience shake my cruel purpose, nor come between that purpose and the execution of the plan."
51. *gall* – bile; bitter substance
52. *sightless* – invisible
53. *mischief* – deeds of evil
54. "And shroud yourself in the darkest smoke of hell."
55. *my* – clear evidence that, at first, Lady Macbeth intends to kill Duncan herself

61. *ignorant* – unknowing (of the future); obscure; inglorious

All that impedes thee from the golden round
Which fate and metaphysical aid doth seem
To have thee crowned withal.

Enter a Messenger.

What is your tidings?
MESSENGER: The King comes here tonight.
LADY MACBETH: Thou art mad to say it!
Is not thy master with him? Who, were it so,
Would have informed for preparation.
MESSENGER: So please you, it is true. Our Thane is coming.
One of my fellows had the speed of him,
Who, almost dead for breath, had scarcely more
Than would make up his message.
LADY MACBETH: Give him tending.
He brings great news.

Exit Messenger.

The raven himself is hoarse
That croaks the fatal entrance of Duncan
Under my battlements. Come, you spirits
That tend on mortal thoughts, unsex me here
And fill me, from the crown to the toe, top-full
Of direst cruelty! Make thick my blood,
Stop up the access and passage to remorse,
That no compunctious visitings of nature
Shake my fell purpose nor keep peace between
The effect and it! Come to my woman's breasts,
And take my milk for gall, you murdering ministers,
Wherever in your sightless substances
You wait on nature's mischief! Come, thick night,
And pall thee in the dunnest smoke of hell
That my keen knife see not the wound it makes
Nor heaven peep through the blanket of the dark
To cry, "Hold, hold!"

Enter Macbeth.

Great Glamis! Worthy Cawdor!
Greater than both, by the all-hail hereafter!
Thy letters have transported me beyond
This ignorant present, and I feel now
The future in the instant.

MACBETH: My dearest love,
Duncan comes here tonight.
LADY MACBETH: And when goes hence?
MACBETH: Tomorrow, as he purposes.
LADY MACBETH: O, never
Shall sun that morrow see!
Your face, my Thane, is as a book where men
May read strange matters. To beguile the time,
Look like the time; bear welcome in your eye,
Your hand, your tongue. Look like the innocent flower,
But be the serpent under it. He that's coming
Must be provided for, and you shall put
This night's great business into my dispatch,
Which shall to all our nights and days to come
Give solely sovereign sway and masterdom.
MACBETH: We will speak further.
LADY MACBETH: Only look up clear.
To alter favour ever is to fear.
Leave all the rest to me.

Exeunt.

69 – 71. "Your face is like an open book. To deceive those around you, welcome them wearing an expression that suits the occasion."

75. *dispatch* – management; futher evidence that Lady Macbeth intends to kill the King herself

80. "To display fear may rouse suspicions."

flower and serpent

Act One
Scene 6

Duncan and his entourage approach Macbeth's castle. They stop to admire the serene surroundings. Lady Macbeth greets them graciously and escorts them into the castle.

Before Macbeth's castle.

Hautboys and torches. Enter King, Malcolm, Donalbain, Banquo, Lennox, Macduff, Ross, Angus, and Attendants.

KING: This castle hath a pleasant seat. The air
Nimbly and sweetly recommends itself
Unto our gentle senses.
BANQUO: This guest of summer,
The temple-haunting martlet, does approve
By his loved mansionry that the heaven's breath
Smells wooingly here. No jutty, frieze,
Buttress, nor coign of vantage, but this bird
Hath made his pendant bed and procreant cradle.
Where they most breed and haunt, I have observed
The air is delicate.

Enter Lady Macbeth.

KING: See, see, our honoured hostess!
The love that follows us sometime is our trouble,
Which still we thank as love. Herein I teach you
How you shall bid God yield us for your pains,
And thank us for your trouble.
LADY MACBETH: All our service
In every point twice done, and then done double,
Were poor and single business to contend
Against those honours deep and broad
Wherewith your Majesty loads our house.
For those of old, and the late dignities
Heaped up to them, we rest your hermits.

hautboy

Stage Direction: *Hautboys* – Musicians enter playing hautboys, which are wooden, double-reed wind instruments.

1. *seat* – site

5. *martlet* – martin. Because this bird's usual nesting grounds are around churches, it can therefore be described as *temple-haunting*.

5. *approve* – proves

8. *coign of vantage* – convenient projecting corner, ideal for observing from

9. "Has made his suspended bed and breeding nest."

15. *yield* – reward. Duncan believes they should be grateful to him for causing inconvenience, because God rewards those who take pains.

KING: Where's the Thane of Cawdor?
We coursed him at the heels and had a purpose
To be his purveyor, but he rides well,
And his great love, sharp as his spur, hath holp him
To his home before us. Fair and noble hostess,
We are your guest tonight.

LADY MACBETH: Your servants ever
Have theirs, themselves, and what is theirs, in compt,
To make their audit at your Highness' pleasure,
Still to return your own.

KING: Give me your hand.
Conduct me to mine host. We love him highly,
And shall continue our graces towards him.
By your leave, hostess.

Exeunt.

19 – 20. "Were feeble service com past services"

23. *your hermits* – tho pray for you

25. *coursed* – rode quick after

26. *purveyor* – one who goes before to make food and lodging preparations for a dignitary

27. *holp* – helped

31. *in compt* – in trust; the King, after all, owns everything

32. *make their audit* – ready to be accounted for and used (for the King's pleasure)

Act One

Scene 7

… whether or … ill the King. … o proceed no … with the plot. … cbeth reproaches … eth for his lack of … . She convinces him to … rough with the plan and assures him that it will appear that Duncan's guards are guilty of the deed.

Stage Direction: *Sewer* – chief server

3. *trammel* – entangle in a net; prevent the occurrence (of the consequences)
4. *surcease* – death

7. *jump* – risk
8. *judgement* – punishment
11 – 12. "offers us drink from cups which we ourselves have poisoned"
14. *Strong both* – both are strong arguments against
17. *faculties* – power
18. *clear* – without fault
20. *taking-off* – murder
22. *Striding the blast* – riding the wind
22. *cherubin* – angels
23. *sightless couriers* – invisible steeds, i.e., the winds
24. *blow* – trumpet, announce

27 – 28. *Vaulting ... other* – bounding ambition which overjumps (the saddle) and falls on the other side (of the horse)

Macbeth's castle.

Hautboys and torches. Enter a Sewer and divers Servants with dishes and service, who pass over the stage. Then enter Macbeth.

Macbeth: If it were done when 'tis done, then 'twere well
It were done quickly. If the assassination
Could trammel up the consequence, and catch,
With his surcease, success, that but this blow
Might be the be-all and the end-all here,
But here, upon this bank and shoal of time,
We'd jump the life to come. But in these cases
We still have judgement here, that we but teach
Bloody instructions, which being taught return
To plague the inventor. This even-handed justice
Commends the ingredients of our poisoned chalice
To our own lips. He's here in double trust:
First, as I am his kinsman and his subject,
Strong both against the deed. Then, as his host,
Who should against his murderer shut the door,
Not bear the knife myself. Besides, this Duncan
Hath borne his faculties so meek, hath been
So clear in his great office, that his virtues
Will plead like angels, trumpet-tongued, against
The deep damnation of his taking-off,
And pity, like a naked new-born babe
Striding the blast, or heaven's cherubin horsed
Upon the sightless couriers of the air,
Shall blow the horrid deed in every eye,
That tears shall drown the wind. I have no spur
To prick the sides of my intent, but only
Vaulting ambition, which overleaps itself
And falls on the other.

Enter Lady Macbeth.

How now, what news?
LADY MACBETH: He has almost supped. Why have you left the chamber?
MACBETH: Hath he asked for me?
LADY MACBETH: Know you not he has?
MACBETH: We will proceed no further in this business.
He hath honoured me of late, and I have bought
Golden opinions from all sorts of people,
Which would be worn now in their newest gloss,
Not cast aside so soon.
LADY MACBETH: Was the hope drunk
Wherein you dressed yourself? Hath it slept since?
And wakes it now, to look so green and pale
At what it did so freely? From this time
Such I account thy love. Art thou afeard
To be the same in thine own act and valour
As thou art in desire? Wouldst thou have that
Which thou esteemest the ornament of life
And live a coward in thine own esteem,
Letting "I dare not" wait upon "I would"
Like the poor cat in the adage?
MACBETH: Prithee, peace!
I dare do all that may become a man.
Who dares do more is none.
LADY MACBETH: What beast was it then
That made you break this enterprise to me?
When you durst do it, then you were a man,
And, to be more than what you were, you would
Be so much more the man. Nor time nor place
Did then adhere, and yet you would make both.
They have made themselves, and that their fitness now
Does unmake you. I have given suck and know
How tender 'tis to love the babe that milks me.
I would, while it was smiling in my face,
Have plucked my nipple from his boneless gums
And dashed the brains out had I so sworn
As you have done to this.
MACBETH: If we should fail?
LADY MACBETH: We fail?
But screw your courage to the sticking-place
And we'll not fail. When Duncan is asleep
(Whereto the rather shall his day's hard journey
Soundly invite him) his two chamberlains

34. *bought* – gained
36. *worn* – enjoyed
38 – 41. "Was your hope (of being king) fed only by drink? Does it wake now to look so sickly at that which you previously desired?"
47. *wait upon* – follow
48. *adage* – familiar saying: "The cat would eat fish, and would not wet her feet." – Thomas Heywood
54. *durst* – dared

56–57. *Nor ... both.* – Some scholars consider this evidence that the Macbeths had discussed killing Duncan before the prophecies of the Weird Sisters. According to Lady Macbeth, an occasion did occur when neither the time nor the place was suitable to assassinate the King, but Macbeth was prepared to do the deed anyway.

RELATED READING

When was the Murder of Duncan First Plotted? – literary essay by A.C. Bradley (page 127)

58. *They ... themselves* – The time and place are opportune

67. "Have courage." Lady Macbeth refers to a bowman tightening the strings on his crossbow tight to the *sticking-place* or the limit it can withstand.

70. *chamberlains* – guards

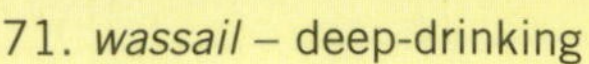

71. *wassail* – deep-drinking

72. *warder* – guardian

73. *fume* – smoke, fog

74. *limbeck* – cap of a still which catches the fumes

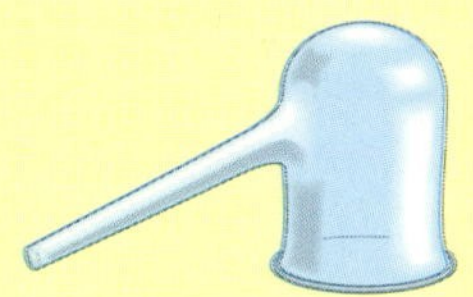

limbeck

78. *spongy* – drunken

79. *quell* – murder

81. *mettle* – spirit

82. *received* – accepted

90. *corporal agent* – physical force

91. *mock the time* – deceive all observers

There once was a king
named Macbeth;
A better king never
drew breath;
The faults of his life
Were all due to his wife
The notorious Lady
Macbeth.
– Anon

Will I with wine and wassail so convince
That memory, the warder of the brain,
Shall be a fume and the receipt of reason
A limbeck only. When in swinish sleep
Their drenched natures lie as in a death,
What cannot you and I perform upon
The unguarded Duncan? What not put upon
His spongy officers, who shall bear the guilt
Of our great quell?

MACBETH: Bring forth men-children only,
For thy undaunted mettle should compose
Nothing but males. Will it not be received,
When we have marked with blood those sleepy two
Of his own chamber and used their very daggers,
That they have done it?

LADY MACBETH: Who dares receive it other,
As we shall make our griefs and clamour roar
Upon his death?

MACBETH: I am settled, and bend up
Each corporal agent to this terrible feat.
Away, and mock the time with fairest show:
False face must hide what the false heart doth know.

Exeunt.

Act One Considerations

ACT ONE **Scene 1**

- If you were directing this scene, what choices would you make with regard to such things as the setting, props, lighting, sound effects, costumes, and acting?

- The last two lines of the scene seem paradoxical. What do you think they mean?

- To be effective, an opening scene must accomplish a variety of purposes. What different functions are served by this first scene? Explain.

ACT ONE **Scene 2**

- One twentieth century film adaptation of the play is called *Throne of Blood* (Japan 1957). The title seems to emphasize one of the more pervasive themes in the play. List as many references to blood as you can in this scene. To what extent are they successful in establishing the atmosphere of the play?

- Although Macbeth does not appear in this scene, we learn a great deal about him. What impressions do we get of Macbeth? Draw as complete a character sketch of Macbeth as you can, based on what people say about him. What do we learn of Duncan's character in this scene?

- The bleeding Sergeant utilizes a number of comparisons to describe the progress of the battle. Choose at least two metaphors which you consider to be especially effective and explain fully the comparisons drawn. Explain why you think the metaphors are effective.

ACT ONE **Scene 3**

- Compare the reactions of Macbeth and Banquo to the witches. J. Dover Wilson believes that Banquo is more interested in the witches themselves than is Macbeth, who seems more interested in the prophecies. To what extent do you agree or disagree with this point of view?

- In line 52, Banquo asks Macbeth why he is startled and seems to fear things that sound so fair. Macbeth has just received excellent news. What could he be thinking that would cause him to react the way he does?

- If you were directing this play, how would you have Macbeth play this particular episode?

- By the end of the scene, Macbeth decides not to kill Duncan and to wait for chance to crown him. What does this emphasize about Macbeth's character? Why is it important to establish this early in the play?

ACT ONE **Scene 4**

- Dramatic irony occurs when the words or actions of a character contain more meaning or significance than is perceived by that character. This device is effective because it places the audience in a superior position of knowledge compared to the character on stage.

  Dramatic irony, when used effectively, can serve to reveal character. Provide examples of dramatic irony in Scene 4. What is revealed about character through the use of this device?

- Duncan is basically a kind and generous King. However, he can be seen as having at least one major shortcoming. What is it? Provide evidence from this scene to support your opinion.

- When Duncan praises Macbeth and Banquo, he relies almost entirely on imagery related to farming and harvesting. What conclusions about Duncan's character and attitudes can we thereby draw?

ACT ONE **Scene 5**

- The opening sentence in Macbeth's letter makes it very clear how he feels about the Weird Sisters. What is his opinion of them? Would he feel this way if he believed they were indeed witches and "instruments of darkness"?

- In the first half of this scene, Lady Macbeth provides the audience with more information about Macbeth's character. What does she say about her husband's character? From what you have learned about Macbeth, would you agree with her estimation?

- An important theme in this play deals with the discrepancy between appearance and reality. The Weird Sisters introduce this theme with their chant that "Fair is foul, and foul is fair." The play is full of echoes of this statement. Review the first five scenes and list all the references that deal with the deceptive nature of appearances. Focus on this scene in particular.

ACT ONE **Scene 6**

- Show how the opening dialogue between Duncan and Banquo depends on dramatic irony for its effect.
- Why is it appropriate that Lady Macbeth's response to Duncan be lavish and humble? What kind of imagery does she use in lines 30 to 33? Why is this appropriate?
- "Where's the Thane of Cawdor?" Where do you think Macbeth is as his wife greets the King at the gate? What is Macbeth thinking and feeling?

ACT ONE **Scene 7**

- In the opening soliloquy, Macbeth offers a number of reasons why it would be wrong to kill Duncan. Outline these reasons by putting the speech into your own words.
- Lady Macbeth uses powerful language in her attempts to deal with her husband's wavering. How does Lady Macbeth persuade her husband to go through with the plan?
- What does this scene reinforce about Lady Macbeth's character?
- How do the last few lines of this scene echo the last words of Act 1, Scene 1?

Act Two

Scene 1

Banquo is tired but cannot sleep. His thoughts revolve around the Weird Sisters' prophecies. He mentions dreaming about the Sisters to Macbeth, but Macbeth denies thinking of them at all. Banquo agrees to discuss the matter further. Macbeth bids Banquo goodnight and proceeds about his bloody business. He imagines a dagger leading him to the place where he is to kill Duncan. The bell signals that all is clear for him to enter Duncan's chamber.

Inverness.

Court of Macbeth's castle.

Enter Banquo, and Fleance, with a torch before him.

BANQUO: How goes the night, boy?
FLEANCE: The moon is down. I have not heard the clock.
BANQUO: And she goes down at twelve.
FLEANCE: I take it 'tis later, sir.
BANQUO: Hold, take my sword.
There's husbandry in heaven,
Their candles are all out. Take thee that too.
A heavy summons lies like lead upon me,
And yet I would not sleep.
Merciful powers, restrain in me the cursed thoughts
That nature gives way to in repose!

Enter Macbeth and a Servant with a torch.

Give me my sword. Who's there?
MACBETH: A friend.
BANQUO: What, sir, not yet at rest? The King's a-bed.
He hath been in unusual pleasure
And sent forth great largess to your offices.
This diamond he greets your wife withal,
By the name of most kind hostess,
And shut up in measureless content.
MACBETH: Being unprepared,
Our will became the servant to defect,
Which else should free have wrought.
BANQUO: All's well.
I dreamt last night of the three Weird Sisters.

6. *husbandry* – thrift; it is cloudy

7. *candles* – stars

16. *largess* – gifts

19. *shut up* – concluded (his comments or his day)

20 – 22. "Had we had more time to prepare, we could have entertained him better."

To you they have showed some truth.
MACBETH: I think not of them;
Yet, when we can entreat an hour to serve,
We would spend it in some words upon that business,
If you would grant the time.
BANQUO: At your kindest leisure.
MACBETH: If you shall cleave to my consent,
When 'tis, it shall make honour for you.
BANQUO: So I lose none
In seeking to augment it, but still keep
My bosom franchised and allegiance clear,
I shall be counselled.
MACBETH: Good repose the while.
BANQUO: Thanks, sir, the like to you.

Exeunt Banquo and Fleance.

MACBETH: Go bid thy mistress, when my drink is ready,
She strike upon the bell. Get thee to bed.

Exit Servant.

Is this a dagger, which I see before me,
The handle toward my hand? Come, let me clutch thee.
I have thee not, and yet I see thee still.
Art thou not, fatal vision, sensible
To feeling as to sight? Or art thou but
A dagger of the mind, a false creation
Proceeding from the heat-oppressed brain?
I see thee yet, in form as palpable
As this which now I draw.
Thou marshalest me the way that I was going,
And such an instrument I was to use.
Mine eyes are made the fools of the other senses,
Or else worth all the rest. I see thee still,
And on thy blade and dudgeon gouts of blood,
Which was not so before. There's no such thing.
It is the bloody business which informs
Thus to mine eyes. Now over the one half-world
Nature seems dead, and wicked dreams abuse
The curtained sleep. Witchcraft celebrates
Pale Hecate's offerings, and withered murder,
Alarumed by his sentinel, the wolf,
Whose howl's his watch, thus with his stealthy pace,
With Tarquin's ravishing strides, towards his design

27. *entreat* – find

31 – 32. "If you are loyal to my cause, when the time comes, it will bring advantage to you."

35. *bosom franchised* – guilt-free conscience

RELATED READING

41. *Macbeth* – poem by Liz Newall (page 150)

44 – 45. *sensible/To feeling* – able to be touched

47. *heat–oppressed* – feverish

dudgeon

54. *dudgeon* – wooden handle

56 – 57. *informs/Thus* – presents this shape

60. *Hecate* – goddess of witchcraft and magic

62. *watch* – signal

Moves like a ghost. Thou sure and firm-set earth,
Hear not my steps, which way they walk, for fear
Thy very stones prate of my whereabout,
And take the present horror from the time,
Which now suits with it. Whiles I threat, he lives.
Words to the heat of deeds too cold breath gives.

A bell rings.

I go, and it is done. The bell invites me.
Hear it not, Duncan, for it is a knell
That summons thee to heaven, or to hell.

Exit.

63. *Tarquin* – tyrant king of Rome whose story is told in Shakespeare's poem *The Rape of Lucrece.* Tarquin ravished the beautiful Lucrece because he was excited by her virtue.

66. *prate* – babble, reveal

69. "Talking cools off the heat associated with action."

"How then, is the hero to be kept from playing the villain's role ... ? The murder, for one thing, is not committed on the stage, though in Elizabethan tragedy it nearly always is. Macbeth, with so little reason, cannot be permitted to kill before our eyes an old man, his sovereign, his guest, his greatest benefactor."
– Elmer Edgar Stoll
(1874 – 1959)
Shakespeare critic

Act Two

Scene 2

Lady Macbeth waits in the courtyard for her husband. A shaken Macbeth appears and informs her that he has done the deed. She is horrified to discover that her husband did not leave the bloody daggers at the murder scene and he refuses to go back to Duncan's chamber. As Lady Macbeth leaves to return the daggers, a loud knocking is heard. When she rejoins Macbeth, they retire to their bedchamber to make it appear that they had been sleeping.

3. *quenched* – put out their fire; caused them to sleep

5. *fatal bellman* – a reference to the town crier or bellman who would ring a bell outside the cell of a condemned man just prior to the execution. This could also be a reference to the bell tolling before a funeral.

6. "And the drunken guards seem to be mocking their duty towards Duncan"

7. *possets* – bedtime drinks

8. *contend* – argue

13. *confounds* – ruins

The same.

Enter Lady Macbeth.

LADY MACBETH: That which hath made them drunk
hath made me bold;
What hath quenched them hath given me fire.
Hark! Peace! It was the owl that shrieked,
The fatal bellman, which gives the sternest good night.
He is about it. The doors are open,
And the surfeited grooms do mock their charge
With snores. I have drugged their possets
That death and nature do contend about them,
Whether they live or die.

MACBETH: *[Within.]* Who's there? What, ho!

LADY MACBETH: Alack, I am afraid they have awaked
And 'tis not done. The attempt and not the deed,
Confounds us. Hark! I laid their daggers ready —
He could not miss them. Had he not resembled
My father as he slept, I had done it.

Enter Macbeth.

My husband!

MACBETH: I have done the deed.
Didst thou not hear a noise?

LADY MACBETH: I heard the owl scream and the crickets cry.
Did not you speak?

MACBETH: When?

LADY MACBETH: Now.

MACBETH: As I descended?

LADY MACBETH: Ay.

MACBETH: Hark! Who lies in the second chamber?

LADY MACBETH: Donalbain.
MACBETH: This is a sorry sight. *[Holding up his bloody hands.]*
LADY MACBETH: A foolish thought, to say a sorry sight.
MACBETH: There's one did laugh in his sleep,
And one cried, "Murder!" that they did wake each other.
I stood and heard them, But they did say their prayers
And addressed them again to sleep.
LADY MACBETH: There are two lodged together.
MACBETH: One cried, "God bless us!" and "Amen" the other,
As they had seen me with these hangman's hands.
Listening their fear, I could not say "Amen,"
When they did say, "God bless us!"
LADY MACBETH: Consider it not so deeply.
MACBETH: But wherefore could not I pronounce "Amen"?
I had most need of blessing, and "Amen" stuck in my throat.
LADY MACBETH: These deeds must not be thought
After these ways. So, it will make us mad.
MACBETH: Methought I heard a voice cry, "Sleep no more!
Macbeth does murder sleep," — the innocent sleep,
Sleep that knits up the ravelled sleave of care,
The death of each day's life, sore labour's bath,
Balm of hurt minds, great nature's second course,
Chief nourisher in life's feast.
LADY MACBETH: What do you mean?
MACBETH: Still it cried, "Sleep no more!" to all the house.
"Glamis hath murdered sleep, and therefore Cawdor
Shall sleep no more. Macbeth shall sleep no more."
LADY MACBETH: Who was it that thus cried? Why, worthy Thane,
You do unbend your noble strength, to think
So brainsickly of things. Go, get some water
And wash this filthy witness from your hand.
Why did you bring these daggers from the place?
They must lie there. Go carry them, and smear
The sleepy grooms with blood.
MACBETH: I'll go no more.
I am afraid to think what I have done.
Look on it again I dare not.
LADY MACBETH: Infirm of purpose!
Give me the daggers. The sleeping and the dead
Are but as pictures. 'Tis the eye of childhood
That fears a painted devil. If he do bleed,
I'll gild the faces of the grooms withal,
For it must seem their guilt.

Exit. Knocking within.

35. *As* – As if

35. Hanging is usually thought of as a bloodless form of execution. However, in Shakespeare's day, a *hangman's hands* would be bloody because hangmen frequently had to draw and quarter those they had just executed.

36. *Listening* – listening to
45. *knits ... care* – unravels tangled threads of life's care
46. *bath* – that which refreshes
47. *Balm* – soothing ointment
47. *second course* – For life to be sustained, two "meals" are essential. The first is food; the second is sleep.
54. *unbend* – weaken
56. *witness* – evidence
66. *painted devil* – picture of devils

72. *Neptune* – Roman god of the oceans

74. *incarnadine* – turn red

MACBETH: Whence is that knocking?
How is it with me, when every noise appals me?
What hands are here? Ha! They pluck out mine eyes!
Will all great Neptune's ocean wash this blood
Clean from my hand? No, this my hand will rather
The multitudinous seas incarnadine,
Making the green one red.

Enter Lady Macbeth.

81 – 82. *constancy ... unattended* – firmness of purpose has abandoned you

85. *watchers* – still awake

LADY MACBETH: My hands are of your colour, but I shame
To wear a heart so white. *[Knock.]*
I hear a knocking at the south entry.
Retire we to our chamber.
A little water clears us of this deed.
How easy is it then! Your constancy
Hath left you unattended. *[Knock.]*
Hark, more knocking.
Get on your nightgown, lest occasion call us
And show us to be watchers. Be not lost
So poorly in your thoughts.
MACBETH: To know my deed,
'Twere best not know myself. *[Knock.]*
Wake Duncan with thy knocking!
I would thou couldst!

Exeunt.

"To mankind in general Macbeth and Lady Macbeth stand out as the supreme type of all that a host and hostess should not be."
– Sir Max Beerbohm (1872 – 1956) British essayist, critic, and cartoonist

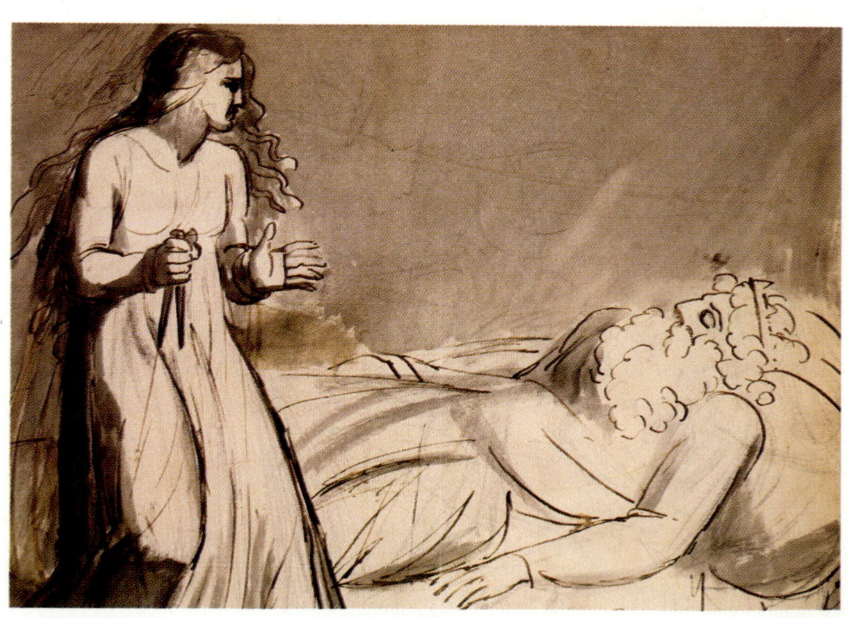

A study of Lady Macbeth and King Duncan by William Blake (1757 – 1827).

Act Two

Scene 3

The Porter's drunken sleep is cut short by the loud knocking of Macduff and Lennox. Macbeth greets the two at the gate. Macduff leaves to rouse the King. A horrified Macduff reports that the King has been murdered. The crime is blamed on the guards, and Macbeth kills the guards out of supposed rage and loyalty for the King. Malcolm and Donalbain, decide to flee the country for their own safety.

The same.

The gate at Macbeth's castle.

Enter a Porter. Knocking [is heard from] within.

Porter: Here's a knocking indeed! If a man were porter of Hell Gate, he should have old turning the key. *[Knock.]* Knock, knock, knock! Who's there, in the name of Belzebub? Here's a farmer that hanged himself on the expectation of plenty. Come in, time-pleaser. Have napkins enow about you. Here you'll sweat for it. *[Knock.]* Knock, knock! Who's there, in the other devil's name? Faith, here's an equivocator that could swear in both the scales against either scale, who committed treason enough for God's sake, yet could not equivocate to heaven. O, come in, equivocator. *[Knock.]* Knock, knock, knock! Who's there? Faith, here's an English tailor come hither for stealing out of a French hose. Come in, tailor. Here you may roast your goose. *[Knock.]* Knock, knock! Never at quiet! What are you? But this place is too cold for hell. I'll devil-porter it no further. I had thought to have let in some of all professions, that go the primrose way to the everlasting bonfire. *[Knock.]* Anon, anon! I pray you, remember the porter.

Opens the gate. Enter Macduff and Lennox.

Macduff: Was it so late, friend, ere you went to bed,
That you do lie so late?
Porter: Faith, sir, we were carousing till the second cock,
And drink, sir, is a great provoker of three things.
Macduff: What three things does drink especially provoke?

3. *Belzebub* – Beelzebub is the name of one of the chief devils; in Hebrew, the name means "Lord of the Flies."

7. *equivocator* – a double-dealer; one who intentionally uses ambiguous words to avoid telling the truth without actually telling a lie. It was argued that a lie is not a lie if the second, true meaning was intended.

8. *scales* – Justice is often represented as holding scales.

21. *second cock* – 3:00 A.M.

24. *nose-painting* – Heavy drinking causes the nose to flush red.

RELATED READING

On the Knocking at the Gate in Macbeth – literary reflection by Thomas De Quincey (page 130)

PORTER: Marry, sir, nose-painting, sleep, and urine. Lechery, sir, it provokes and unprovokes. It provokes the desire, but it takes away the performance. Therefore much drink may be said to be an equivocator with lechery. It makes him, and it mars him; it sets him on, and it takes him off; it persuades him and disheartens him; makes him stand to and not stand to. In conclusion, equivocates him in a sleep, and giving him the lie, leaves him.

MACDUFF: I believe, drink gave thee the lie last night.

PORTER: That it did, sir, in the very throat on me, but I requited him for his lie, and, I think, being too strong for him, though he took up my legs sometime, yet I made a shift to cast him.

MACDUFF: Is thy master stirring?

Enter Macbeth.

Our knocking has awaked him. Here he comes.

LENNOX: Good morrow, noble sir.

MACBETH: Good morrow, both.

MACDUFF: Is the King stirring, worthy Thane?

MACBETH: Not yet.

MACDUFF: He did command me to call timely on him.
I have almost slipped the hour.

MACBETH: I'll bring you to him.

MACDUFF: I know this is a joyful trouble to you,
But yet 'tis one.

40. *Not yet.* – the second-best example of understatement in the play

41. *timely* – early

"Excepting the disgusting passage of the Porter, which I dare pledge myself to demonstrate as interpolation of the actors, I do not remember in *Macbeth* a single pun or play on words."
– Samuel Taylor Coleridge (1772 – 1834) British Romantic poet

Macbeth: The labour we delight in physics pain.
This is the door.
Macduff: I'll make so bold to call, for 'tis my limited service.

Exit Macduff.

Lennox: Goes the King hence today?
Macbeth: He does — he did appoint so.
Lennox: The night has been unruly.
Where we lay, our chimneys were blown down,
And, as they say, lamentings heard in the air,
Strange screams of death,
And, prophesying with accents terrible
Of dire combustion and confused events,
New hatched to the woeful time,
The obscure bird clamoured the livelong night.
Some say the earth was feverous
And did shake.
Macbeth: 'Twas a rough night.
Lennox: My young remembrance cannot parallel
A fellow to it.

Enter Macduff.

Macduff: O horror! Horror! Horror!
Tongue nor heart cannot conceive nor name thee!
Macbeth and **Lennox:** What's the matter?

46. *physics* – eases; treats (as in cures)
48. *limited* – appointed
55. *accents terrible* – terrifying voices
56. *dire combustion* – civil confusion, uproar
58. *obscure bird* – owl
61. *'Twas a rough night* – the best example of understatement in the play

67. *Confusion* – destruction

69. *Lord's anointed temple* – a reference to the King, who is anointed with oil during the coronation ceremony and invested by divine right to rule over the country

74. *Gorgon* – In Greek mythology, the Gorgon was a monster so hideous that its very sight turned people to stone.

78. *counterfeit* – imitation

80. *great doom's image* – picture of Doomsday or Judgment Day

82. *countenance* – look upon; face

84. *parley* – a military meeting announced by a trumpet call

Gorgon

98. *mortality* – human life

MACDUFF: Confusion now hath made his masterpiece!
Most sacrilegious murder hath broke ope
The Lord's anointed temple and stole thence
The life of the building.
MACBETH: What is it you say? The life?
LENNOX: Mean you his Majesty?
MACDUFF: Approach the chamber and destroy your sight
With a new Gorgon. Do not bid me speak.
See, and then speak yourselves. Awake, awake!

Exeunt Macbeth and Lennox.

Ring the alarum bell. Murder and treason!
Banquo and Donalbain! Malcolm, awake!
Shake off this downy sleep, death's counterfeit,
And look on death itself! Up, up, and see
The great doom's image! Malcolm! Banquo!
As from your graves rise up and walk like sprites
To countenance this horror! Ring the bell.

Bell rings. Enter Lady Macbeth.

LADY MACBETH: What's the business,
That such a hideous trumpet calls to parley
The sleepers of the house? Speak, speak!
MACDUFF: O gentle lady,
'Tis not for you to hear what I can speak.
The repetition in a woman's ear
Would murder as it fell.

Enter Banquo.

O Banquo, Banquo! Our royal master's murdered.
LADY MACBETH: Woe, alas!
What, in our house?
BANQUO: Too cruel anywhere.
Dear Duff, I prithee, contradict thyself,
And say it is not so.

Enter Macbeth, Lennox, and Ross.

MACBETH: Had I but died an hour before this chance,
I had lived a blessed time, for from this instant
There's nothing serious in mortality.
All is but toys. Renown and grace is dead,

The wine of life is drawn, and the mere lees
Is left this vault to brag of.

Enter Malcolm and Donalbain.

DONALBAIN: What is amiss?
MACBETH: You are, and do not know it.
The spring, the head, the fountain of your blood
Is stopped, the very source of it is stopped.
MACDUFF: Your royal father's murdered.
MALCOLM: O, by whom?
LENNOX: Those of his chamber, as it seemed, had done it.
Their hands and faces were all badged with blood.
So were their daggers, which unwiped we found
Upon their pillows. They stared, and were distracted.
No man's life was to be trusted with them.
MACBETH: O, yet I do repent me of my fury,
That I did kill them.
MACDUFF: Wherefore did you so?
MACBETH: Who can be wise, amazed, temperate and furious,
Loyal and neutral, in a moment? No man.
The expedition of my violent love
Outrun the pauser, reason. Here lay Duncan,
His silver skin laced with his golden blood,
And his gashed stabs looked like a breach in nature
For ruin's wasteful entrance. There, the murderers,
Steeped in the colours of their trade, their daggers
Unmannerly breeched with gore. Who could refrain,
That had a heart to love, and in that heart
Courage to make his love known?
LADY MACBETH: Help me hence, ho!
MACDUFF: Look to the lady.
MALCOLM: *[Aside to Donalbain.]* Why do we hold our tongues,
That most may claim this argument for ours?
DONALBAIN: *[Aside to Malcolm.]* What should be spoken here,
Where our fate, hid in an auger hole,
May rush and seize us? Let's away,
Our tears are not yet brewed.
MALCOLM: *[Aside to Donalbain.]* Nor our strong sorrow
Upon the foot of motion.
BANQUO: Look to the lady.

Lady Macbeth is carried out.

100. *lees* – dregs; sediment found at the bottom of a bottle of wine
101. *vault* – earth; wine cellar or vault (to continue the wine metaphor)

109. *badged* – marked

118. *expedition* – haste

122. *wasteful* – destructive

124. *breeched* – covered

129 – 130. "Why are we silent when we should have the most to say on this subject?"
132. *fate* – death
auger hole – tiny hole made with a very sharp point (perhaps of a dagger)
134. *brewed* – ready (to flow)
136. "Has begun to express itself"

138. "When we are dressed"

141. *scruples* – doubts

147. *briefly* – quickly

158. "The closer we are in blood (family relationship to Duncan), the more likely we are to be murdered also."

162. *dainty* – formal, particular

163. *shift away* – slip off secretly

warrant – justification

And when we have our naked frailties hid,
That suffer in exposure, let us meet
And question this most bloody piece of work
To know it further. Fears and scruples shake us.
In the great hand of God I stand, and thence
Against the undivulged pretense I fight
Of treasonous malice.

foil to Lady macbeth

MACDUFF: And so do I.

ALL: So all.

MACBETH: Let's briefly put on manly readiness
And meet in the hall together.

ALL: Well contented.

Exeunt all but Malcolm and Donalbain.

MALCOLM: What will you do?
Let's not consort with them.
To show an unfelt sorrow is an office
Which the false man does easy.
I'll to England.

DONALBAIN: To Ireland, I.
Our separated fortune shall keep us both the safer.
Where we are, there's daggers in men's smiles.
The near in blood, the nearer bloody.

MALCOLM: This murderous shaft that's shot
Hath not yet lighted, and our safest way
Is to avoid the aim. Therefore to horse,
And let us not be dainty of leave-taking,
But shift away. There's warrant in that theft
Which steals itself when there's no mercy left.

Exeunt.

malcom + donalbain upon finding the king dead fled which looks suspicious, so people suspected them and that they hired the guards to kill Duncan. macduff however is not totaly convinced and is suspicious of macbeth who now is to be crowned king of scottland.

Act Two
Scene 4

Before Macbeth's castle.

Enter Ross and an Old Man.

OLD MAN: Threescore and ten I can remember well,
Within the volume of which time I have seen
Hours dreadful and things strange, but this sore night
Hath trifled former knowings.
ROSS: Ha, good father,
Thou seest the heavens, as troubled with man's act,
Threaten his bloody stage. By the clock 'tis day,
And yet dark night strangles the travelling lamp.
Is it night's predominance, or the day's shame,
That darkness does the face of earth entomb,
When living light should kiss it?
OLD MAN: 'Tis unnatural,
Even like the deed that's done. On Tuesday last
A falcon towering in her pride of place
Was by a mousing owl hawked at and killed.
ROSS: And Duncan's horses
(A thing most strange and certain)
Beauteous and swift, the minions of their race,
Turned wild in nature, broke their stalls, flung out,
Contending 'gainst obedience, as they would
Make war with mankind.
OLD MAN: 'Tis said they eat each other.
ROSS: They did so,
To the amazement of mine eyes that looked upon it.

Enter Macduff.

Here comes the good Macduff.
How goes the world, sir, now?

An Old Man and Ross, recounting the unnatural events that transpired during the night of Duncan's murder, are joined by Macduff who informs them that suspicion of the murder has fallen on the King's sons. It is believed that Malcolm and Donalbain hired the two guards to do the deed. Macbeth has been chosen as the new King. Ross leaves to attend the coronation but Macduff chooses to return home to Fife instead.

3. *sore* – grievous; dreadful

6 – 7. Another theatre metaphor. The Earth is the *bloody stage* and the *heavens* is the roof of the stage.

12. *'Tis unnatural.* – The Elizabethans believed that when the natural order of the universe is violated at the highest level (such as through the assassination of a king), the natural world is thrown into chaos and reflects this violation through events such as comets, earthquakes, famine, disease, eclipses, etc.

18. *minions* – best

32. *suborned* – bribed; induced
37. "Self–defeating ambition that will devour greedily"
40. *Scone* – traditional site where Scottish kings are crowned. See map on page 8.
41. *invested* – crowned

throne of Scone

50. "In case we find that things were more comfortable during the old days (under Duncan) than they are nowadays (under Macbeth)."
52. *benison* – blessing
53. *would make* – work to make

RELATED READING

The Macbeth Murder Mystery – short story by James Thurber (page 132)

MACDUFF: Why, see you not?
ROSS: Is it known who did this more than bloody deed?
MACDUFF: Those that Macbeth hath slain.
ROSS: Alas, the day!
What good could they pretend?
MACDUFF: They were suborned.
Malcolm and Donalbain, the King's two sons,
Are stolen away and fled, which puts upon them
Suspicion of the deed.
ROSS: 'Gainst nature still!
Thriftless ambition, that wilt ravin up
Thine own life's means! Then 'tis most like
The sovereignty will fall upon Macbeth.
MACDUFF: He is already named, and gone to Scone
To be invested.
ROSS: Where is Duncan's body?
MACDUFF: Carried to Colme-kill,
The sacred storehouse of his predecessors
And guardian of their bones.
ROSS: Will you to Scone?
MACDUFF: No, cousin, I'll to Fife.
ROSS: Well, I will thither.
MACDUFF: Well, may you see things well done there. Adieu,
Lest our old robes sit easier than our new!
ROSS: Farewell, father.
OLD MAN: God's benison go with you and with those
That would make good of bad and friends of foes!

Exeunt.

Act Two Considerations

ACT TWO **Scene 1**

- When Banquo remarks that the night is especially dark, we can conclude that nature is somehow reflecting what is going on in the affairs of people. The dark night, in other words, reflects Macbeth's dark desires. This is an example of *pathetic fallacy.* What atmosphere is created through the use of this device in this scene? As you read the rest of the play, pay attention to the use of pathetic fallacy and the resultant mood or atmosphere.

  What movies, novels or short stories can you think of that contain examples of pathetic fallacy?

- What purpose does the scene between Macbeth and Banquo serve? What evidence is there that Banquo is suspicious of Macbeth?

- In Macbeth's aside in Act 1 Scene 3, beginning on line 140, we learn that Macbeth has an overactive imagination. To him, "Present fears/Are less than horrible imaginings." How would you describe Macbeth's state of mind as he makes his way to Duncan's chambers?

- If you were directing this scene, would you have an actual dagger floating in the air? Why or why not?

ACT TWO Scene 2

- What evidence is there that Lady Macbeth is not as strong as she would like to believe? What does she warn Macbeth the dangers are of thinking too deeply on their deeds?

- Shakespeare chooses to have Duncan murdered offstage. Consider the reasons why. Perhaps you can respond by writing a prose description of the murder. Attempt this using the third person omniscient point of view and then the first person point of view. How do these versions differ?

- In Act 1 Scene 5, Lady Macbeth suggests that she would kill Duncan herself. Why does she change her mind? What does this emphasize about her character?

- What sentiment does Macbeth express at the end of this scene? What does this reveal about Macbeth's character? Why would it be necessary to emphasize this point?

ACT TWO Scene 3

- How does the night as described by Lennox compare with the night as experienced by the Macbeths in the previous scene?

- Compare how Macbeth behaves in this scene with his behaviour in the previous scene.

- Lady Macbeth takes centre stage twice in this scene. What do her actions reveal about her character? To answer this question, you will need to decide if she genuinely faints or if she is putting on an act to divert attention away from Macbeth.

- Imagine you are Macbeth and it is a short time after the events of this scene. Write a dialogue in which you explain to Lady Macbeth why you killed the two guards.

- What evidence is there at the end of this scene that Malcolm is unwilling to put on appearances for the sake of the Scottish Lords?

ACT TWO **Scene 4**

- The Elizabethans believed that when the natural order of the universe is violated, nature reflects the disorder and is thrown into chaos. List the various unnatural events that occur before and after the murder of Duncan.

- Macduff refuses to go to Scone to see Macbeth crowned. What reasons would he have for his decision? What are your first impressions of Macduff based on this scene and the previous one?

Act Three
Scene 1

Banquo, although he suspects that Macbeth has attained the crown through foul play, is heartened by the Weird Sisters' prophecy that he himself will father a line of kings. Macbeth appears and learns of Banquo's plans for that day. Macbeth orders Banquo not to miss the banquet that evening. Alone, Macbeth is reminded of the prophecy concerning Banquo's line. Two Murderers join Macbeth, who proceeds to persuade them to kill Banquo and Fleance.

Forres.

The palace.

Enter Banquo.

BANQUO: Thou hast it now — King, Cawdor, Glamis, all,
As the Weird Women promised, and I fear
Thou play'dst most foully for it. Yet it was said
It should not stand in thy posterity,
But that myself should be the root and father
Of many kings. If there come truth from them
(As upon thee, Macbeth, their speeches shine),
Why, by the verities on thee made good,
May they not be my oracles as well
And set me up in hope? But hush, no more.

Sennet sounds. Enter Macbeth as King, Lady [Macbeth], Lennox, Ross, Lords, and Attendants.

MACBETH: Here's our chief guest.
LADY MACBETH: If he had been forgotten,
It had been as a gap in our great feast
And all-thing unbecoming.
MACBETH: Tonight we hold a solemn supper, sir,
And I'll request your presence.
BANQUO: Let your Highness
Command upon me, to the which my duties
Are with a most indissoluble tie
For ever knit.
MACBETH: Ride you this afternoon?
BANQUO: Ay, my good lord.

7. *shine* – show favour, speak true

Stage Direction: *Sennet* – trumpet call.

Stage Direction: *Lady Macbeth* – The Folio clearly indicates that it is Lady Lennox and not Lady Macbeth who enters with Macbeth in this scene. Most editors consider this an error and substitute Lady Macbeth.

14. *all-thing* – everything

15. *solemn supper* – state banquet

19. *indissoluble* – that which cannot be broken

MACBETH: We should have else desired your good advice,
(Which still hath been both grave and prosperous)
In this day's council — but we'll take tomorrow.
Is it far you ride!

BANQUO: As far, my lord, as will fill up the time
'Twixt this and supper. Go not my horse the better,
I must become a borrower of the night
For a dark hour or twain.

MACBETH: Fail not our feast.

BANQUO: My lord, I will not.

MACBETH: We hear our bloody cousins are bestowed
In England and in Ireland, not confessing
Their cruel parricide, filling their hearers
With strange invention. But of that tomorrow,
When therewithal we shall have cause of state
Craving us jointly. Hie you to horse.
Adieu, till you return at night.
Goes Fleance with you?

BANQUO: Ay, my good lord. Our time does call upon us.

MACBETH: I wish your horses swift and sure of foot,
And so I do commend you to their backs.
Farewell.

Exit Banquo.

Let every man be master of his time
Till seven at night. To make society
The sweeter welcome,
We will keep ourself till supper time alone.
While then, God be with you!

Exeunt all but Macbeth and a Servant.

Sirrah, a word with you. Attend those men
Our pleasure?

SERVANT: They are, my lord, without the palace gate.

MACBETH: Bring them before us.

Exit Servant.

To be thus is nothing, but to be safely thus.
Our fears in Banquo stick deep,
And in his royalty of nature reigns
That which would be feared. 'Tis much he dares,
And to that dauntless temper of his mind,

29 – 30. "I will have to make use of one or two hours of darkness to complete my ride."

35. *parricide* – murder of one's father

36. *strange invention* – ridiculous lies

"If Macduff, with no knowledge of the weird sisters, can suspect Macbeth so actively as to refuse his presence at the coronation, then for Banquo, with his knowledge, to have nothing more than a vague fear is for him to be naive almost to the point of imbecility."
– Isaac Asimov (1920 – 1992) American science and science fiction writer

46 – 47. "To make having company all the more pleasant"

50. *Attend* – await

52. *without* – just outside

58. *dauntless temper* – fearless quality

He hath a wisdom that doth guide his valour
To act in safety. There is none but he
Whose being I do fear. And under him
My Genius is rebuked, as it is said
Mark Antony's was by Caesar. He chid the Sisters
When first they put the name of King upon me
And bade them speak to him; then prophet-like
They hailed him father to a line of kings.
Upon my head they placed a fruitless crown
And put a barren sceptre in my gripe,
Thence to be wrenched with an unlineal hand,
No son of mine succeeding. If it be so,
For Banquo's issue have I filed my mind,
For them the gracious Duncan have I murdered,
Put rancours in the vessel of my peace
Only for them, and mine eternal jewel
Given to the common enemy of man,
To make them kings, the seed of Banquo kings!
Rather than so, come, Fate, into the list,
And champion me to the utterance!
Who's there?

Enter Servant, with two Murderers.

Now go to the door and stay there till we call.

Exit Servant.

Was it not yesterday we spoke together?

First murderer: It was, so please your Highness.

Macbeth: Well then,
Now have you considered of my speeches?
Know that it was he, in the times past,
Which held you so under fortune,
Which you thought had been our innocent self?
This I made good to you in our last conference,
Passed in probation with you
How you were borne in hand, how crossed,
The instruments, who wrought with them,
And all things else that might
To half a soul and to a notion crazed
Say, "Thus did Banquo."

First murderer: You made it known to us.

Macbeth: I did so,
And went further, which is now

62. *Genius* – guardian spirit

63. *Caesar* – This reference is to Octavius Caesar, who was Julius Caesar's nephew and heir. Octavius ultimately defeated Antony and established the Roman Empire.

68. *gripe* – grip; grasp

69. *unlineal* – not of the family line

71. *filed* – defiled

73. *rancours* – bitterness

74. *eternal jewel* – immortal soul

75. *common ... man* – the devil, Satan

77. *list* – place of battle, tournament arena

78. *utterance* – the end, to death

89. *passed in probation* – went over the evidence

90. *borne in hand* – deceived

91. *wrought with* – used

93. *notion* – mind

Our point of second meeting.
Do you find your patience so predominant
In your nature, that you can let this go?
Are you so gospelled, to pray for this good man
And for his issue, whose heavy hand
Hath bowed you to the grave and beggared
Yours forever?

First murderer: We are men, my liege.

Macbeth: Ay, in the catalogue ye go for men,
As hounds and greyhounds, mongrels, spaniels, curs,
Shoughs, water-rugs, and demi-wolves are clept
All by the name of dogs. The valued file
Distinguishes the swift, the slow, the subtle,
The housekeeper, the hunter, every one
According to the gift which bounteous nature
Hath in him closed, whereby he does receive
Particular addition, from the bill
That writes them all alike; and so of men.
Now if you have a station in the file,
Not in the worst rank of manhood, say it,
And I will put that business in your bosoms
Whose execution takes your enemy off,
Grapples you to the heart and love of us,
Who wear our health but sickly in his life,
Which in his death were perfect.

Second murderer: I am one, my liege,
Whom the vile blows and buffets of the world
Have so incensed that I am reckless what I do
To spite the world.

First murderer: And I another
So weary with disasters, tugged with fortune,
That I would set my life on any chance,
To mend it or be rid on it.

Macbeth: Both of you know Banquo was your enemy.

Both murderers: True, my lord.

Macbeth: So is he mine, and in such bloody distance
That every minute of his being thrusts
Against my nearest of life, and though I could
With barefaced power sweep him from my sight
And bid my will avouch it, yet I must not,
For certain friends that are both his and mine,
Whose loves I may not drop, but wail his fall
Who I myself struck down. And thence it is
That I to your assistance do make love,
Masking the business from the common eye
For sundry weighty reasons.

106. *catalogue* – list of things
108. "Shaggy dogs, water-dogs, and half-wolves are called"
109. *valued file* – list that features a ranking
113. *closed* – enclosed; set (as in a jewel setting)
114. *addition* – distinction; quality
116. *station* – placing
128. *tugged* – scuffled; pulled about by
135. *nearest of life* – heart (the most vital part of one's body)
137. *avouch* – justify
139. *wail his fall* – lament his death

SECOND MURDERER: We shall, my lord,
Perform what you command us.
FIRST MURDERER: Though our lives —
MACBETH: Your spirits shine through you.
Within this hour at most
I will advise you where to plant yourselves,
Acquaint you with the perfect spy of the time,
The moment on it, for it must be done tonight
And something from the palace (always thought
That I require a clearness) and with him,
To leave no rubs nor botches in the work,
Fleance his son, that keeps him company,
Whose absence is no less material to me
Than is his father's, must embrace the fate
Of that dark hour. Resolve yourselves apart;
I'll come to you anon.
BOTH MURDERERS: We are resolved, my lord.
MACBETH: I'll call upon you straight. Abide within.

Exeunt Murderers.

It is concluded. Banquo, thy soul's flight,
If it find heaven, must find it out tonight.

Exit.

150. *perfect ... time* – most up–to–date information (as to when to do it)
152. *always thought* – it being thought
153. *clearness* – freedom from suspicion or complicity
154. *rubs* – impediments (a bowling term)
156. *material* – important
158. *Resolve ... apart* – Take some private time to decide whether you want to do this or not.

Lady Macbeth learns from a servant that Banquo is gone from the court. Alone, she admits that attaining the throne has not resulted in happiness or peace of mind. Macbeth enters and he too reveals that his mind has been tortured with fears of Banquo. They resolve to put on happy faces for the banquet that evening. Macbeth hints of some deed of dreadful note that he has undertaken but does not share with his wife the details of the plan.

Act Three

Scene 2

Macbeth's palace.

Enter Lady Macbeth and a Servant.

LADY MACBETH: Is Banquo gone from court?
SERVANT: Ay, madam, but returns again tonight.
LADY MACBETH: Say to the King I would attend his leisure
For a few words.
SERVANT: Madam, I will.

Exit.

LADY MACBETH: Nought's had, all's spent,
Where our desire is got without content.
'Tis safer to be that which we destroy
Than by destruction dwell in doubtful joy.

Enter Macbeth.

How now, my lord? Why do you keep alone,
Of sorriest fancies your companions making,
Using those thoughts which should indeed have died
With them they think on? Things without all remedy
Should be without regard. What's done is done.
MACBETH: We have scorched the snake, not killed it.
She'll close and be herself, whilst our poor malice
Remains in danger of her former tooth.
But let the frame of things disjoint,
Both the worlds suffer,
Ere we will eat our meal in fear and sleep
In the affliction of these terrible dreams
That shake us nightly. Better be with the dead,
Whom we, to gain our peace, have sent to peace,

6. "Nothing has been gained; everything has been lost."

12. *Using* – consorting with

15. *scorched* – cut, gashed

16. *poor malice* – feeble plottings

18 – 19. "Let the universe fall apart and both heaven and earth suffer"

Than on the torture of the mind to lie
In restless ecstasy.
Duncan is in his grave,
After life's fitful fever he sleeps well.
Treason has done his worst. Nor steel, nor poison,
Malice domestic, foreign levy, nothing,
Can touch him further.

LADY MACBETH: Come on,
Gentle my lord, sleek over your rugged looks.
Be bright and jovial among your guests tonight.

MACBETH: So shall I, love, and so, I pray, be you.
Let your remembrance apply to Banquo.
Present him eminence, both with eye and tongue.
Unsafe the while, that we must lave
Our honours in these flattering streams
And make our faces vizards to our hearts,
Disguising what they are.

LADY MACBETH: You must leave this.

MACBETH: O, full of scorpions is my mind, dear wife!
Thou knowest that Banquo and his Fleance lives.

LADY MACBETH: But in them nature's copy is not eterne.

MACBETH: There's comfort yet. They are assailable.
Then be thou jocund. Ere the bat hath flown
His cloistered flight, ere to black Hecate's summons
The shard-borne beetle with his drowsy hums
Hath rung night's yawning peal,
There shall be done a deed of dreadful note.

LADY MACBETH: What's to be done?

MACBETH: Be innocent of the knowledge, dearest chuck,
Till thou applaud the deed. Come, seeling night,
Scarf up the tender eye of pitiful day,
And with thy bloody and invisible hand
Cancel and tear to pieces that great bond
Which keeps me pale! Light thickens,
And the crow makes wing to the rooky wood.
Good things of day begin to droop and drowse,
Whiles night's black agents to their preys do rouse.
Thou marvellest at my words, but hold thee still.
Things bad begun make strong themselves by ill.
So, prithee, go with me.

Exeunt.

25. *ecstasy* – strong emotion; frenzy

32. *sleek* – smooth

35. *remembrance* – considerations

36. *eminence* – highest rank

37. *lave* – wash

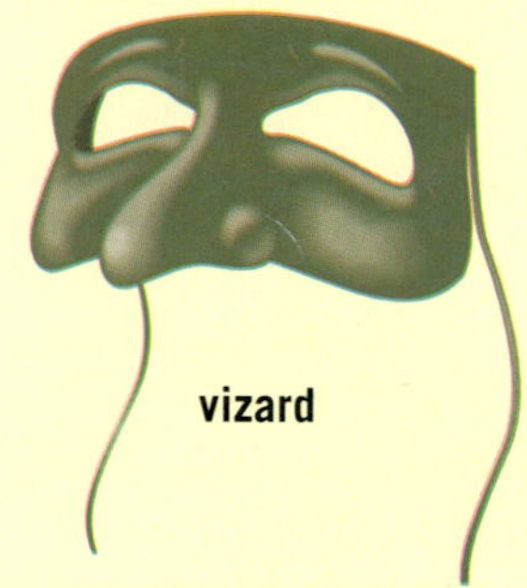

39. *vizards* – masks

44. "Nature did not make them in a form immortal."

45. *assailable* – open to attack

46. *jocund* – cheerful

53. *seeling* – a falconry term: to tame a falcon, the owner would seel or sew its eyelids shut; blinding

54. *scarf up* – blindfold (as with a scarf)

56. *bond* – i.e., Banquo's life and the Weird Sisters' prophecy about Banquo

58. *rooky* – full of rooks or crows

62. "Evil deeds gather strength through more evil deeds."

Act Three
Scene 3

Macbeth sends a third murderer to help kill Banquo and Fleance. The three ambush their prey and manage to kill Banquo. In the confusion, however, Fleance escapes.

A park near the palace.

Enter three Murderers.

FIRST MURDERER: But who did bid thee join with us?
THIRD MURDERER: Macbeth.
SECOND MURDERER: He needs not our mistrust, since he delivers
Our offices and what we have to do
To the direction just.
FIRST MURDERER: Then stand with us.
The west yet glimmers with some streaks of day;
Now spurs the lated traveller apace
To gain the timely inn, and near approaches
The subject of our watch.
THIRD MURDERER: Hark! I hear horses.
BANQUO: *[Within.]* Give us a light there, ho!
SECOND MURDERER: Then 'tis he!
The rest that are within the note of expectation
Already are in the court.
FIRST MURDERER: His horses go about.
THIRD MURDERER: Almost a mile, but he does usually —
So all men do — from hence to the palace gate
Make it their walk.
SECOND MURDERER: A light, a light!

Enter Banquo, and Fleance with a torch.

THIRD MURDERER: 'Tis he.
FIRST MURDERER: Stand to it.
BANQUO: It will be rain tonight.
FIRST MURDERER: Let it come down.

They set upon Banquo.

3 – 5. Spoken to First Murderer. "We need not mistrust him (Third Murderer) since he has accurate knowledge of our orders."

8. *lated* – belated; tardy
9. *timely* – on time

14. *note of expectation* – list of expected guests (at Macbeth's banquet)
16. *go about* – go around the long way

RELATED READING

Macbeth as the Third Murderer – literary conjecture by Harold C. Goddard (page 136)

BANQUO: O, treachery!
Fly, good Fleance, fly, fly, fly!
Thou mayst revenge. O slave!

Dies. Fleance escapes.

THIRD MURDERER: Who did strike out the light?
FIRST MURDERER: Was it not the way?
THIRD MURDERER: There's but one down. The son is fled.
SECOND MURDERER: We have lost
Best half of our affair.
FIRST MURDERER: Well, let's away and say how much is done.

Exeunt.

"[Macbeth] was a poet with his brain – the greatest poet that Shakespeare has ever drawn – and a villain with his heart. . . . All through the play his darkest deeds are heralded by high thoughts told in the most glorious word painting, so that, after a little, the reader or hearer comes to understand that excellence of poetic thought is but a suggestion of the measure of the wickedness that is to follow."
– Sir Henry Irving (1838 – 1905) famous British Shakespearean actor

The banquet is well underway when one of the murderers appears and reports to Macbeth. Macbeth is delighted with the news that Banquo is dead but is dismayed to learn that Fleance has escaped. When Macbeth rejoins the party, he loses all composure in front of his guests when he sees Banquo's ghost. Lady Macbeth asks the guests to leave. Macbeth announces his intention to visit the Weird Sisters to get more information.

1. *degrees* – rank (and therefore places at the table)
6. *state* – official chair of state (with a canopy)

state chair

21. *nonpareil* – without equal

25. *else* – otherwise

Act Three
Scene 4

A Hall in the palace.

A banquet prepared. Enter Macbeth, Lady Macbeth, Ross, Lennox, Lords, and Attendants.

MACBETH: You know your own degrees, sit down.
At first and last the hearty welcome.
LORDS: Thanks to your Majesty.
MACBETH: Ourself will mingle with society
And play the humble host.
Our hostess keeps her state, but in best time
We will require her welcome.
LADY MACBETH: Pronounce it for me, sir, to all our friends,
For my heart speaks they are welcome.

Enter First Murderer to the door.

MACBETH: See, they encounter thee with their hearts' thanks.
Both sides are even. Here I'll sit in the midst.
Be large in mirth. Anon we'll drink a measure
The table round. *[Approaches the Murderer at the door.]*
There's blood upon thy face.
MURDERER: 'Tis Banquo's then.
MACBETH: 'Tis better thee without than he within.
Is he dispatched?
MURDERER: My lord, his throat is cut. That I did for him.
MACBETH: Thou art the best of the cut-throats!
Yet he's good that did the like for Fleance.
If thou didst it, thou art the nonpareil.
MURDERER: Most royal sir,
Fleance is 'scaped.
MACBETH: *[Aside.]* Then comes my fit again.
I had else been perfect,

Whole as the marble, founded as the rock,
As broad and general as the casing air.
But now I am cabined, cribbed, confined, bound in
To saucy doubts and fears — But Banquo's safe?

MURDERER: Ay, my good lord. Safe in a ditch he bides,
With twenty trenched gashes on his head,
The least a death to nature.

MACBETH: Thanks for that.
There the grown serpent lies. The worm that's fled
Hath nature that in time will venom breed,
No teeth for the present. Get thee gone. Tomorrow
We'll hear ourselves again.

Exit Murderer.

LADY MACBETH: My royal lord,
You do not give the cheer. The feast is sold
That is not often vouched, while 'tis amaking,
'Tis given with welcome. To feed were best at home.
From thence the sauce to meat is ceremony;
Meeting were bare without it.

Enter the Ghost of Banquo and sits in Macbeth's place.

MACBETH: Sweet remembrancer!
Now good digestion wait on appetite,
And health on both!

LENNOX: May it please your Highness sit.

MACBETH: Here had we now our country's honour roofed,
Were the graced person of our Banquo present,
Who may I rather challenge for unkindness
Than pity for mischance!

ROSS: His absence, sir,
Lays blame upon his promise. Please it your Highness
To grace us with your royal company?

MACBETH: The table's full.

LENNOX: Here is a place reserved, sir.

MACBETH: Where?

LENNOX: Here, my good lord. What is it that moves your
Highness?

MACBETH: Which of you have done this?

LORDS: What, my good lord?

MACBETH: Thou canst not say I did it. Never shake
Thy gory locks at me.

ROSS: Gentlemen, rise. His Highness is not well.

27. "As free and unconfined as the surrounding sky"

31. *trenched* – cut

39 – 43. "You do not give the toast. If the host does not frequently give the welcome to his guests, the meal is like one that is paid for in a public eating place. Simple dining is fine when home without company. What makes dinner parties special are the ceremonies. Dinner parties would be nothing without ceremonies and courtesies."

48 – 49. "We would have all the noblest men in the country under one roof if Banquo were also present."
50. *challenge for* – accuse of

"A number of Shakespearean revisionists now believe that Macbeth spied the ghost of Banquo at the banquet not out of guilt, but as a result of having just dined on haggis." The recipe for haggis includes: "Sheep's lungs, heart and liver, mixed with suet, oats and seasonings – all boiled in the animal's stomach."
– Mark Starr – American professor of English

68. *extend* – prolong

73. *painting* – creation; representation

75. *flaws* – sudden gusts of wind; outbursts of passion

77. *woman's story* – old wife's tale

78. *Authorized* – on the authority or word of

78. *Shame itself* – Shame on you

84. *charnel houses* – places where bones of the dead are stored

84 – 86. "If the dead insist on returning to haunt the living, we will have to let birds of prey eat the bodies that are usually housed in sepulchres."

LADY MACBETH: Sit, worthy friends. My lord is often thus,
And hath been from his youth. Pray you, keep seat.
The fit is momentary. Upon a thought
He will again be well. If much you note him,
You shall offend him and extend his passion.
Feed, and regard him not — Are you a man?

MACBETH: Ay, and a bold one, that dare look on that
Which might appal the devil.

LADY MACBETH: O proper stuff!
This is the very painting of your fear.
This is the air-drawn dagger which you said
Led you to Duncan. O, these flaws and starts,
(Impostors to true fear) would well become
A woman's story at a winter's fire,
Authorized by her grandam. Shame itself!
Why do you make such faces? When all's done,
You look but on a stool.

MACBETH: Prithee, see there!
Behold! Look! Lo! How say you?
Why, what care I? If thou canst nod, speak too.
If charnel houses and our graves must send
Those that we bury back, our monuments
Shall be the maws of kites.

Exit Ghost.

Lady macbeth: What, quite unmanned in folly?
Macbeth: If I stand here, I saw him.
Lady macbeth: Fie, for shame!
Macbeth: Blood hath been shed ere now, in the olden time,
Ere humane statute purged the gentle weal.
Ay, and since too, murders have been performed
Too terrible for the ear. The time has been,
That, when the brains were out, the man would die,
And there an end! But now they rise again,
With twenty mortal murders on their crowns,
And push us from our stools. This is more strange
Than such a murder is.
Lady macbeth: My worthy lord,
Your noble friends do lack you.
Macbeth: I do forget.
Do not muse at me, my most worthy friends.
I have a strange infirmity, which is nothing
To those that know me. Come, love and health to all!
Then I'll sit down. Give me some wine, fill full.

Enter Ghost.

I drink to the general joy of the whole table,
And to our dear friend Banquo, whom we miss.
Would he were here! To all and him we thirst,
And all to all.
Lords: Our duties and the pledge.

91. "Before human laws freed society from constant conflict."

111. *Avaunt* – Get out!

113. *speculation* – sight

120. *Hyrcan tiger* – symbol of ferocity

123 – 124. "Challenge me to single combat in an isolated place. If I trembling stay at home (i.e., refuse to fight) then accuse me of being a baby girl."

133. *You ... strange* – You cause me to doubt (my own nature)

148. "Gravestones have been known to move and whispers from trees have revealed the names of murderers."

MACBETH: Avaunt, and quit my sight! Let the earth hide thee!
Thy bones are marrowless, thy blood is cold;
Thou hast no speculation in those eyes
Which thou dost glare with.
LADY MACBETH: Think of this, good peers,
But as a thing of custom. 'Tis no other.
Only it spoils the pleasure of the time.
MACBETH: What man dare, I dare.
Approach thou like the rugged Russian bear,
The armed rhinoceros, or the Hyrcan tiger,
Take any shape but that, and my firm nerves
Shall never tremble. Or be alive again,
And dare me to the desert with thy sword.
If trembling I inhabit then, protest me
The baby of a girl. Hence, horrible shadow!
Unreal mockery, hence!

Exit Ghost.

Why, so, being gone,
I am a man again. Pray you sit still.
LADY MACBETH: You have displaced the mirth,
Broke the good meeting with most admired disorder.
MACBETH: Can such things be,
And overcome us like a summer's cloud,
Without our special wonder? You make me strange
Even to the disposition that I owe
When now I think you can behold such sights
And keep the natural ruby of your cheeks
When mine is blanched with fear.
ROSS: What sights, my lord?
LADY MACBETH: I pray you, speak not. He grows worse and worse.
Question enrages him. At once, good night.
Stand not upon the order of your going,
But go at once.
LENNOX: Good night, and better health
Attend his Majesty!
LADY MACBETH: A kind good night to all!

Exeunt Lords.

MACBETH: It will have blood, they say.
Blood will have blood.
Stones have been known to move and trees to speak;

Augures and understood relations have
By maggot pies and choughs and rooks brought forth
The secretest man of blood. What is the night?

Lady macbeth: Almost at odds with morning, which is which.

Macbeth: How sayest thou, that Macduff denies his person
At our great bidding?

Lady macbeth: Did you send to him, sir?

Macbeth: I hear it by the way, but I will send.
There's not a one of them but in his house
I keep a servant fee'd. I will tomorrow,
(And betimes I will) to the Weird Sisters.
More shall they speak, for now I am bent to know,
By the worst means, the worst. For mine own good
All causes shall give way. I am in blood
Stepped in so far that, should I wade no more,
Returning were as tedious as go over.
Strange things I have in head that will to hand,
Which must be acted ere they may be scanned.

Lady macbeth: You lack the season of all natures, sleep.

Macbeth: Come, we'll to sleep. My strange and self-abuse
Is the initiate fear that wants hard use.
We are yet but young in deed.

Exeunt.

149. *Augures ... relations* – Those who can read signs or omens know the relationship between things that do not appear to have any connection to each other.
150. *maggot-pies ... rooks* – magpies and jackdaws (a type of crow) and crows
151. *man of blood* – murderer
152. "As close as one can get to morning."
158. *servant fee'd* – spy; paid informer
159. *betimes* – very early
165. *will to hand* – will be done
166. *scanned* – thought about
167. *season* – preservative
168. *self–abuse* – deception
169. "The fear felt by a beginner will lessen through action and practice."

"At the most, the only potency the witches have in the drama is the power from within Macbeth, and not from without. It is subjective only, and it is the power over him of his own belief in the supernatural, and not the operation of an actual outside supernatural spell or witchcraft."
– H.M. Doak, *The Supernatural in Macbeth*

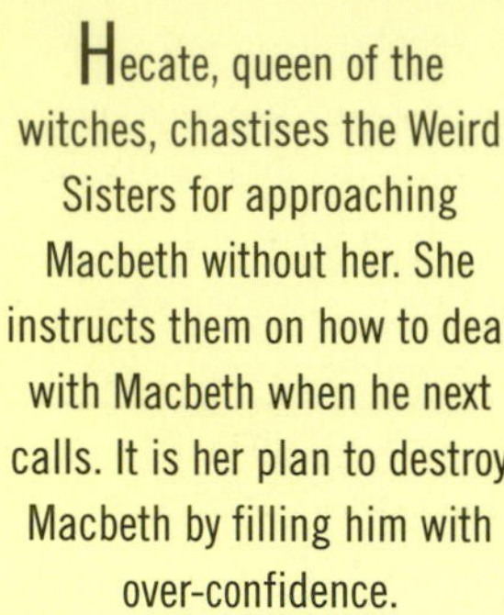

Hecate, queen of the witches, chastises the Weird Sisters for approaching Macbeth without her. She instructs them on how to deal with Macbeth when he next calls. It is her plan to destroy Macbeth by filling him with over-confidence.

Act Three

Scene 5

A heath.

Thunder. Enter the three Witches, meeting Hecate.

FIRST WITCH: Why, how now, Hecate? You look angerly.
HECATE: Have I not reason, beldams as you are,
Saucy and overbold? How did you dare
To trade and traffic with Macbeth
In riddles and affairs of death,
And I, the mistress of your charms,
The close contriver of all harms,
Was never called to bear my part,
Or show the glory of our art?
And, which is worse, all you have done
Hath been but for a wayward son,
Spiteful and wrathful, who, as others do,
Loves for his own ends, not for you.
But make amends now. Get you gone,
And at the pit of Acheron
Meet me in the morning. Thither he
Will come to know his destiny.
Your vessels and your spells provide,
Your charms and everything beside.
I am for the air. This night I'll spend
Unto a dismal and a fatal end.
Great business must be wrought ere noon.
Upon the corner of the moon
There hangs a vaporous drop profound.
I'll catch it ere it come to ground,
And that distilled by magic sleights
Shall raise such artificial sprites
As by the strength of their illusion
Shall draw him on to his confusion.

2. *beldams* – hags
3. *Saucy* – rude and insolent
15. *Acheron* – river in Hades
21. *dismal ... end* – disastrous and deadly purpose
24. *profound* – hidden qualities or powers
26. *sleights* – spells
27. *sprites* – spirits

He shall spurn fate, scorn death, and bear
His hopes above wisdom, grace, and fear.
And you all know security
Is mortals' chiefest enemy.

Music and a song within, "Come away, come away."

Hark! I am called. My little spirit, see,
Sits in a foggy cloud and stays for me.

Exit.

FIRST WITCH: Come, let's make haste. She'll soon be
Back again.

Exeunt.

Many scholars believe this scene was written by Thomas Middleton and not Shakespeare. In fact, the song sung by the witches at the end of the scene, "Come Away, Come Away," comes from Middleton's play *The Witch*.

With unrestrained sarcasm, Lennox and another Lord discuss recent events in Scotland. They are convinced that Macbeth is responsible for the murders of Duncan and Banquo, and they are glad that Malcolm and Donalbain are beyond Macbeth's reach. Macduff has fled to England to join up with Malcolm, who is mustering a military force to rid Scotland of Macbeth's bloody tyranny.

Act Three
Scene 6

Forres.

The palace.

Enter Lennox and another Lord.

Lennox: My former speeches
Have but hit your thoughts,
Which can interpret farther, only I say
Thing's have been strangely borne. The gracious Duncan
Was pitied of Macbeth — marry, he was dead.
And the right valiant Banquo walked too late —
Whom, you may say, if it please you, Fleance killed,
For Fleance fled. Men must not walk too late.
Who cannot want the thought, how monstrous
It was for Malcolm and for Donalbain
To kill their gracious father? Damned fact!
How it did grieve Macbeth! Did he not straight,
In pious rage, the two delinquents tear
That were the slaves of drink and thralls of sleep?
Was not that nobly done? Ay, and wisely too,
For 'twould have angered any heart alive
To hear the men deny it. So that, I say,
He has borne all things well, and I do think
That, had he Duncan's sons under his key
(As, and it please heaven, he shall not) they should find
What 'twere to kill a father. So should Fleance.
But, peace! For from broad words, and 'cause he failed
His presence at the tyrant's feast, I hear,
Macduff lives in disgrace. Sir, can you tell
Where he bestows himself?

Lord: The son of Duncan,
From whom this tyrant holds the due of birth,

3. *interpret farther* – go on to draw your own conclusions

9. *Who ... thought* – who would not conclude

13. *delinquents* – the guards who had failed in their duty and slept

14. *thralls* – slaves; captives

20. *and it* – if it

22. *broad* – plain; outspoken

27. *due of birth* – birthright, i.e., the kingship

Lives in the English court and is received
Of the most pious Edward with such grace
That the malevolence of fortune nothing
Takes from his high respect. Thither Macduff
Is gone to pray the holy King, upon his aid
To wake Northumberland and warlike Siward,
That by the help of these, (with Him above
To ratify the work) we may again
Give to our tables meat, sleep to our nights,
Free from our feasts and banquets bloody knives,
Do faithful homage, and receive free honours —
All which we pine for now. And this report
Hath so exasperate the King that he
Prepares for some attempt of war.

Lennox: Sent he to Macduff?

Lord: He did, and with an absolute "Sir, not I,"
The cloudy messenger turns me his back,
And hums, as who should say, "You'll rue the time
That clogs me with this answer."

Lennox: And that well might
Advise him to a caution, to hold what distance
His wisdom can provide. Some holy angel
Fly to the court of England and unfold
His message ere he come, that a swift blessing
May soon return to this our suffering country
Under a hand accursed!

Lord: I'll send my prayers with him.

Exeunt.

30. *malevolence of fortune* – misfortune

32. *upon his aid* – with his support

38. *faithful homage* – loyalty (to the proper king)

44. *cloudy* – frowning, sullen

46. *clogs* – burdens. The messenger realizes that reporting this response will not get him a reward from Macbeth.

Act Three Considerations

ACT THREE **Scene 1**

- Paraphrase Banquo's opening soliloquy. What does this speech reveal about his character?

- Shakespeare scholar A.C. Bradley considers Banquo to be a silent accomplice of Macbeth. According to Holinshed's *Chronicles,* Banquo was indeed an accomplice in the killing of Duncan. Do you agree with Bradley? To what extent does Banquo's silence serve to assist Macbeth in his attaining of the crown?

- Outline all the reasons that Macbeth offers as to why Banquo must be killed. What else does Macbeth's soliloquy reveal about his state of mind?

- Rather than simply ordering the murderers to kill Banquo, Macbeth converses with them at length. Why? Create a diary entry in which one of the murderers reviews their discussions with Macbeth.

- How does the planning of Banquo's murder compare with that of Duncan's murder? What change in Macbeth's character does this emphasize?

ACT THREE **Scene 2**

- This scene emphasizes that neither of the Macbeths are happy after attaining the crown. What reasons are suggested for their unhappiness?

- Describe the relationship between the Macbeths as revealed in this scene. Who appears stronger and more in control?

- It appears obvious that Macbeth has not involved his wife in the planning of Banquo's murder. Write a diary entry in which Macbeth explains why he wants Lady Macbeth to be innocent of the knowledge till she can applaud the deed.

ACT THREE **Scene 3**

- Macbeth had promised the murderers that he would send the "perfect spy of the time" to them. Read this scene carefully and comment on whether or not the Third Murderer deserves this title. In other words, how much does he know about Banquo and his habits?

- When Fleance flees at the end of this scene, he does not return to Macbeth's castle. Would he have any reason not to? Imagine you are Fleance. Explain your reasons to a friend or family member for not returning to Macbeth's castle.

ACT THREE **Scene 4**

- This scene marks the beginning of Macbeth's downfall. List the various "defeats" suffered by Macbeth during this scene.

- Consider the irony of the entrance of Banquo's ghost. In previous scenes, what has foreshadowed Banquo's appearance at the banquet?

- If you were the director, would the ghost be visible to the audience or would it be, as Lady Macbeth suggests, a figment of Macbeth's imagination? What are the advantages and disadvantages of making the ghost visible?

- Compare the behaviour of the two Macbeths during this scene. Imagine you were a guest at the banquet. Describe what you saw to a friend or family member.

ACT THREE **Scene 5**

- Few scholars believe that this scene was written by Shakespeare. Nevertheless, it does provide us with certain information concerning Macbeth's fate. What does Hecate's speech reveal?

- Imagine you are involved in a production of the play and that the director has chosen to cut this scene from the performance. Write a defence of or a challenge to this decision. What would be gained or lost by dropping this scene?

ACT THREE **Scene 6**

- In pairs, using as sarcastic a tone of voice as you both can, read aloud the dialogue between the two characters in this scene. What evidence is there in the speeches that would suggest that this scene should be read sarcastically?
- What information does the Lord reveal concerning Macduff and Macbeth?
- Who do you think will be Macbeth's next victim(s)? What evidence would suggest this?
- What is the dramatic purpose of this short scene?

Act Four

Scene 1

The Weird Sisters, huddled around a boiling cauldron, prepare a spell. Macbeth appears and demands information. A series of apparitions appear and Macbeth is heartened by their encouraging prophecies. The apparitions and the Weird Sisters disappear. Lennox arrives and reports that Macduff has fled to England. Macbeth resolves to attack Macduff's castle and have everyone within killed.

A cavern.

In the middle, a boiling cauldron.
Thunder. Enter the three Witches.

FIRST WITCH: Thrice the brinded cat hath mewed.
SECOND WITCH: Thrice and once the hedge-pig whined.
THIRD WITCH: Harpier cries, "'Tis time, 'tis time."
FIRST WITCH: Round about the cauldron go;
In the poisoned entrails throw.
Toad, that under cold stone
Days and nights has thirty-one
Sweltered venom sleeping got,
Boil thou first in the charmed pot.
ALL: Double, double, toil and trouble,
Fire burn and cauldron bubble.
SECOND WITCH: Fillet of a fenny snake,
In the cauldron boil and bake;
Eye of newt and toe of frog,
Wool of bat and tongue of dog,
Adder's fork and blind-worm's sting,
Lizard's leg and howlet's wing,
For a charm of powerful trouble,
Like a hell-broth boil and bubble.
ALL: Double, double, toil and trouble,
Fire burn and cauldron bubble.
THIRD WITCH: Scale of dragon, tooth of wolf,
Witch's mummy, maw and gulf
Of the ravined salt-sea shark,
Root of hemlock digged in the dark,
Liver of blaspheming Jew,
Gall of goat and slips of yew
Slivered in the moon's eclipse,

1. *brinded* – streaked
3. *Harpier* – likely the familiar of the third witch, perhaps an owl. The name Harpier may be a variation on the word "harpy."
12. *fenny* – from the marshes or fens
16. *fork* – forked tongue
16. *blind worm* – small lizard, supposedly blind and poisonous
17. *howlet* – small owl
23. *maw and gulf* – stomach and gullet
24. *ravined* – ravenous
27. *yew* – a tree that was commonly found in churchyards. The entire tree was considered poisonous.

29. Turks and Tartars were considered unbaptized and therefore valued by the witches.

31. *drab* – prostitute
33. *chaudron* – entrails

Nose of Turk and Tartar's lips,
Finger of birth-strangled babe
Ditch-delivered by a drab,
Make the gruel thick and slab.
Add thereto a tiger's chaudron,
For the ingredients of our cauldron.

ALL: Double, double, toil and trouble,
Fire burn and cauldron bubble.

SECOND WITCH: Cool it with a baboon's blood,
Then the charm is firm and good.

Enter Hecate and other witches.

RELATED READING

At the Fire and Cauldron Health-Food Restaurant – poem by Martin Robbins (page 144)

HECATE: O, well done! I commend your pains,
And everyone shall share in the gains.
And now about the cauldron sing,
Like elves and fairies in a ring,
Enchanting all that you put in.

Music and a song, "Black spirits."
[Exit Hecate.]

SECOND WITCH: By the pricking of my thumbs,
Something wicked this way comes.
Open, locks, whoever knocks!

Enter Macbeth.

MACBETH: How now, you secret, black, and midnight hags?
What is it you do?

ALL: A deed without a name.

MACBETH: I conjure you, by that which you profess
(However you come to know it) answer me.
Though you untie the winds and let them fight
Against the churches, though the yesty waves
Confound and swallow navigation up,
Though bladed corn be lodged and trees blown down,
Though castles topple on their warders' heads,
Though palaces and pyramids do slope
Their heads to their foundations, though the treasure
Of nature's germens tumble all together
Even till destruction sicken, answer me
To what I ask you.

FIRST WITCH: Speak.

SECOND WITCH: Demand.

52 – 53. *fight ... churches* – blow down the steeples
53. *yesty* – frothy, yeasty

59. *germens* – seeds; that which germinates. Macbeth is willing to see the seeds of all things not yet created mixed together and destroyed. In other words, his own personal happiness and peace of mind are more important to him than all creation.

THIRD WITCH: We'll answer.
FIRST WITCH: Say, if thou'dst rather hear it from our mouths,
    Or from our masters?
MACBETH: Call 'em. Let me see 'em.
FIRST WITCH: Pour in sow's blood that hath eaten
    Her nine farrow. Grease that's sweaten
    From the murderer's gibbet, throw
    Into the flame.
ALL: Come, high or low;
    Thyself and office deftly show!

Thunder. First Apparition, an armed Head.

MACBETH: Tell me, thou unknown power —
FIRST WITCH: He knows thy thought.
    Hear his speech, but say thou nought.
FIRST APPARITION: Macbeth! Macbeth! Macbeth!
    Beware Macduff,
    Beware the Thane of Fife. Dismiss me. Enough.

Descends.

MACBETH: Whatever thou art, for thy good caution, thanks!
    Thou hast harped my fear aright. But one word more —
FIRST WITCH: He will not be commanded. Here's another,
    More potent than the first.

Thunder. Second Apparition, a bloody Child.

SECOND APPARITION: Macbeth! Macbeth! Macbeth!
MACBETH: Had I three ears, I'd hear thee.
SECOND APPARITION: Be bloody, bold, and resolute.
    Laugh to scorn
    The power of man, for none of woman born
    Shall harm Macbeth.

Descends.

MACBETH: Then live, Macduff. What need I fear of thee?
    But yet I'll make assurance double sure,
    And take a bond of Fate. Thou shalt not live,
    That I may tell pale-hearted fear it lies,
    And sleep in spite of thunder.

69. "Her litter of piglets. Grease that's perspired"
70. *gibbet* – gallows

gibbet

72. *high or low* – in rank; or from the higher or lower regions
73. *office* – function, task

90 – 91. Macbeth assumes that the words of the second apparition cancel out those of the first.

92. *bond* – guarantee of security
94. *in ... thunder* – soundly

96 – 97. *the round/And top* – royal crown

100. *chafes* – is angry

105. *impress* – conscript into military service

106. *bodements* – predictions

109. *lease of nature* – normal life span

109 – 110. *pay ... custom* – die in old age

Thunder. Third Apparition, a Child crowned, with a tree in his hand.

What is this, that rises like the issue of a King,
And wears upon his baby brow the round
And top of sovereignty?

ALL: Listen, but speak not to it.

THIRD APPARITION: Be lion-mettled, proud, and take no care
Who chafes, who frets, or where conspirers are.
Macbeth shall never vanquished be, until
Great Birnam Wood to high Dunsinane Hill
Shall come against him.

Descends.

MACBETH: That will never be.
Who can impress the forest, bid the tree
Unfix his earth-bound root? Sweet bodements, good!
Rebellion's head, rise never till the Wood
Of Birnam rise, and our high-placed Macbeth
Shall live the lease of nature, pay his breath
To time and mortal custom. Yet my heart
Throbs to know one thing. Tell me, if your art
Can tell so much, shall Banquo's issue ever
Reign in this kingdom?

ALL: Seek to know no more.

Macbeth: I will be satisfied! Deny me this,
And an eternal curse fall on you! Let me know.
Why sinks that cauldron, and what noise is this?

Hautboys.

First witch: Show!
Second witch: Show!
Third witch: Show!
All: Show his eyes, and grieve his heart!
Come like shadows, so depart!

A show of eight Kings, and Banquo last, with a glass in his hand.

Macbeth: Thou are too like the spirit of Banquo. Down!
Thy crown does sear mine eyeballs. And thy hair,
Thou other gold-bound brow, is like the first.
A third is like the former. Filthy hags!
Why do you show me this? A fourth! Start, eyes!
What, will the line stretch out to the crack of doom?
Another yet! A seventh! I'll see no more!
And yet the eighth appears, who bears a glass
Which shows me many more; and some I see
That twofold balls and treble sceptres carry.
Horrible sight! Now I see 'tis true;
For the blood-boltered Banquo smiles upon me,
And points at them for his. What, is this so?

RELATED READING

James I – poem by Rudyard Kipling (page 139)

130. *glass* – mirror

134. *blood–boltered* – hair matted with blood

First witch: Ay, sir, all this is so. But why
Stands Macbeth thus amazedly?
Come, sisters, cheer we up his sprites,
And show the best of our delights.
I'll charm the air to give a sound,
While you perform your antic round,
That this great King may kindly say
Our duties did his welcome pay.

Music. The Witches dance, and vanish.

Macbeth: Where are they? Gone?
Let this pernicious hour
Stand aye accursed in the calendar!
Come in, without there!

Enter Lennox.

Lennox: What's your Grace's will?
Macbeth: Saw you the Weird Sisters?
Lennox: No, my lord.
Macbeth: Came they not by you?
Lennox: No indeed, my lord.
Macbeth: Infected be the air whereon they ride,
And damned all those that trust them! I did hear
The galloping of horse. Who was it came by?
Lennox: 'Tis two or three, my lord, that bring you word
Macduff is fled to England.
Macbeth: Fled to England?
Lennox: Ay, my good lord.
Macbeth: *[Aside.]* Time, thou anticipatest my dread
exploits.
The flighty purpose never is overtook
Unless the deed go with it. From this moment
The very firstlings of my heart shall be
The firstlings of my hand. And even now,
To crown my thoughts with acts, be it thought and done!
The castle of Macduff I will surprise,
Seize upon Fife, give to the edge of the sword
His wife, his babes, and all unfortunate souls
That trace him in his line. No boasting like a fool!
This deed I'll do before this purpose cool.
But no more sights! — Where are these gentlemen?
Come, bring me where they are.

Exeunt.

141. *antic round* – fantastic dance

146. *aye* – ever

"... *Macbeth* which, though I have seen it often, yet it is one of the best plays for a stage, and variety of dancing and musique, that ever I saw."
– Samuel Pepys (1633 – 1703) English diarist

163. *firstlings ... hand* – no sooner thought about but they shall be acted upon

Act Four

Scene 2

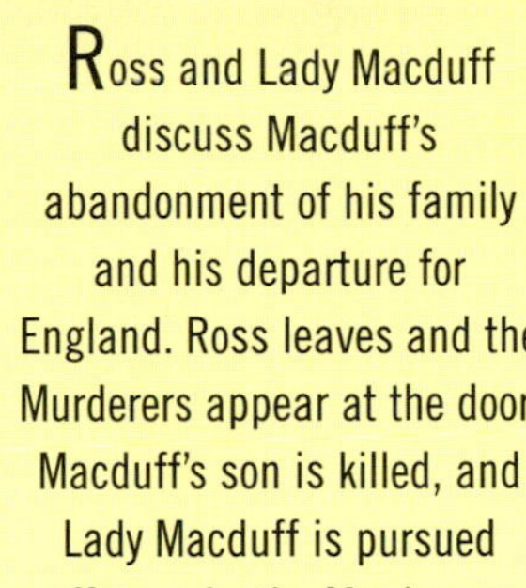
Ross and Lady Macduff discuss Macduff's abandonment of his family and his departure for England. Ross leaves and the Murderers appear at the door. Macduff's son is killed, and Lady Macduff is pursued offstage by the Murderers.

Fife.

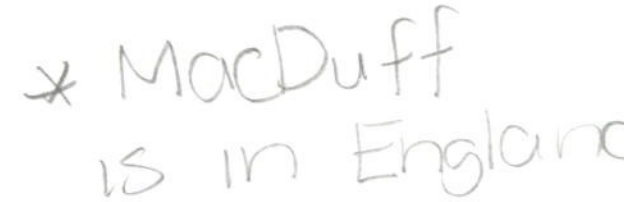

Macduff's castle.

Enter Lady Macduff, her Son, and Ross.

LADY MACDUFF: What had he done, to make him fly the land?
ROSS: You must have patience, madam.
LADY MACDUFF: He had none.
His flight was madness. When our actions do not,
Our fears do make us traitors.
ROSS: You know not
Whether it was his wisdom or his fear.
LADY MACDUFF: Wisdom? To leave his wife, to leave his babes,
His mansion, and his titles, in a place
From whence himself does fly? He loves us not —
He wants the natural touch. For the poor wren,
The most diminutive of birds, will fight,
Her young ones in her nest, against the owl.
All is the fear and nothing is the love,
As little is the wisdom, where the flight
So runs against all reason.
ROSS: My dearest coz,
I pray you, school yourself. But for your husband,
He is noble, wise, judicious, and best knows
The fits of the season. I dare not speak much further,
But cruel are the times when we are traitors
And do not know ourselves. When we hold rumour
From what we fear, yet know not what we fear,
But float upon a wild and violent sea
Each way and move. I take my leave of you.
Shall not be long but I'll be here again.
Things at the worst will cease or else climb upward

RELATED READING

A Scene Left Out of Shakespeare's Macbeth – scene from William Davenant's treatment of *Macbeth* (page 140)

11. *wants* – lacks

18. *school* – control

20. *fits of the season* – the way things are and what needs to be done

21 – 22. *when ... ourselves.* – when we are said to be traitors and do not know that we are so

22. *hold* – accept

23. *From what* – on the basis of what

33. *my disgrace* – perhaps because he is about to weep

35. With Ross's departure, the audience is treated to the second of only two comic scenes in the play. The touching comic bantering between the boy and his mother serves as the calm before the storm.

41. *lime* – sticky substance used to catch birds
42. *gin* – snare
44. *Poor birds* – emphasis on *poor,* as opposed to rich. Traps are not set for poor (unimportant) birds.

To what they were before. My pretty cousin,
Blessing upon you!
LADY MACDUFF: Fathered he is,
And yet he's fatherless.
ROSS: I am so much a fool, should I stay longer
It would be my disgrace and your discomfort.
I take my leave at once.

Exit.

LADY MACDUFF: Sirrah, your father's dead.
And what will you do now? How will you live?
SON: As birds do, Mother.
LADY MACDUFF: What, with worms and flies?
SON: With what I get, I mean, and so do they.
LADY MACDUFF: Poor bird!
Thou wouldst never fear the net nor lime,
The pitfall nor the gin.
SON: Why should I, Mother?
Poor birds they are not set for.
My father is not dead, for all your saying.
LADY MACDUFF: Yes, he is dead.
How wilt thou do for father?
SON: Nay, how will you do for a husband?
LADY MACDUFF: Why, I can buy me twenty at any market.
SON: Then you'll buy them to sell again.
LADY MACDUFF: Thou speakest with all thy wit,
And yet, in faith, with wit enough for thee.
SON: Was my father a traitor, Mother?
LADY MACDUFF: Ay, that he was.
SON: What is a traitor?
LADY MACDUFF: Why one that swears and lies.
SON: And be all traitors that do so?
LADY MACDUFF: Everyone that does so is a traitor
And must be hanged.
SON: And must they all be hanged that swear and lie?
LADY MACDUFF: Everyone.
SON: Who must hang them?
LADY MACDUFF: Why, the honest men.
SON: Then the liars and swearers are fools, for there are liars and swearers enow to beat the honest men and hang up them.
LADY MACDUFF: Now, God help thee, poor monkey!
But how wilt thou do for a father?
SON: If he were dead, you'd weep for him. If you

would not, it were a good sign that I should quickly
have a new father.

LADY MACDUFF: Poor prattler, how thou talkst!

Enter a Messenger.

MESSENGER: Bless you, fair dame! I am not to you known,
Though in your state of honour I am perfect.
I doubt some danger does approach you nearly.
If you will take a homely man's advice,
Be not found here. Hence, with your little ones.
To fright you thus, methinks I am too savage.
To do worse to you were fell cruelty,
Which is too nigh your person. Heaven preserve you!
I dare abide no longer.

Exit.

LADY MACDUFF: Whither should I fly?
I have done no harm. But I remember now
I am in this earthly world, where to do harm
Is often laudable, to do good sometime
Accounted dangerous folly. Why then, alas,
Do I put up that womanly defense,
To say I have done no harm? —
What are these faces?

Enter Murderers.

MURDERER: Where is your husband?

LADY MACDUFF: I hope, in no place so unsanctified
Where such as thou may'st find him.

MURDERER: He's a traitor.

SON: Thou liest, thou shag-eared villain!

MURDERER: What, you egg!

[Stabs him.]

Young fry of treachery!

SON: He has killed me, Mother.
Run away, I pray you! *[Dies.]*

Exit Lady Macduff, crying "Murder!" pursued by the Murderers.

74. *state ... perfect* – perfectly aware of your status

75. *doubt* – suspect; fear

76. *homely* – humble

79. "Not to tell you would be more cruel"

80. *too nigh* – too nearly upon

85. *laudable* – praiseworthy

Act Four

Scene 3

Macduff has arrived in England and attempts to convince Malcolm to lead a military force to overthrow Macbeth. Malcolm suspects that Macduff has been sent by Macbeth, but once Malcolm is convinced that Macduff is indeed loyal, he pledges to do all he can to restore peace and legitimate rule to Scotland. Ross arrives and reports the slaughter of Macduff's family and household. Malcolm encourages Macduff to convert his grief to anger and to seek revenge.

England.

Before the King's palace.

Enter Malcolm and Macduff.

MALCOLM: Let us seek out some desolate shade and there
Weep our sad bosoms empty.
MACDUFF: Let us rather
Hold fast the mortal sword, and like good men
Bestride our downfallen birthdom. Each new morn
New widows howl, new orphans cry, new sorrows
Strike heaven on the face, that it resounds
As if it felt with Scotland and yelled out
Like syllable of dolour.
MALCOLM: What I believe, I'll wail;
What know, believe; and what I can redress,
As I shall find the time to friend, I will.
What you have spoke, it may be so perchance.
This tyrant, whose sole name blisters our tongues,
Was once thought honest. You have loved him well.
He hath not touched you yet. I am young, but something
You may deserve of him through me, and wisdom
To offer up a weak, poor, innocent lamb
To appease an angry god.
MACDUFF: I am not treacherous.
MALCOLM: But Macbeth is.
A good and virtuous nature may recoil
In an imperial charge. But I shall crave your pardon.
That which you are, my thoughts cannot transpose.
Angels are bright still, though the brightest fell.
Though all things foul would wear the brows of grace,
Yet grace must still look so.

4. *mortal* – deadly
5. *bestride* – defend

9. *like syllable* – similar cries

17. "You may get something by betraying me"

22 – 23. *recoil ... charge* – yield to a royal command
25. *the brightest* – (of angels) Lucifer. The name "Lucifer" means the "bright one."

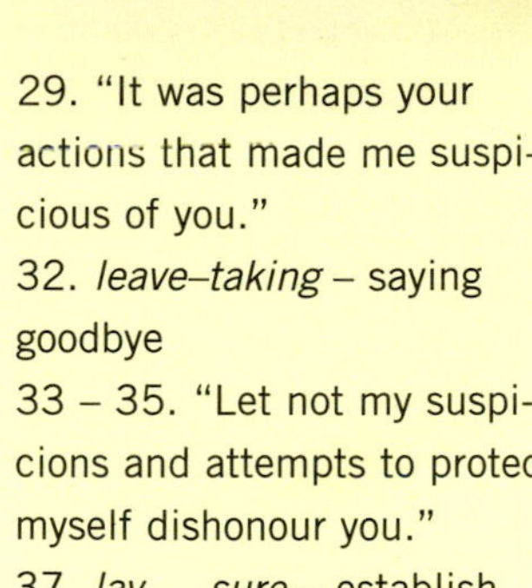

MACDUFF: I have lost my hopes.
MALCOLM: Perchance even there where I did find my doubts.
Why in that rawness left you wife and child,
Those precious motives, those strong knots of love,
Without leave-taking? I pray you,
Let not my jealousies be your dishonours,
But mine own safeties. You may be rightly just,
Whatever I shall think.
MACDUFF: Bleed, bleed, poor country!
Great tyranny, lay thou thy basis sure,
For goodness dare not check thee. Wear thou thy wrongs.
The title is affeered. Fare thee well, Lord.
I would not be the villain that thou thinkest
For the whole space that's in the tyrant's grasp
And the rich East to boot.
MALCOLM: Be not offended.
I speak not as in absolute fear of you.
I think our country sinks beneath the yoke.
It weeps, it bleeds, and each new day a gash
Is added to her wounds. I think, withal
There would be hands uplifted in my right,
And here from gracious England have I offer
Of goodly thousands. But for all this,
When I shall tread upon the tyrant's head,
Or wear it on my sword, yet my poor country
Shall have more vices than it had before,
More suffer and more sundry ways than ever,
By him that shall succeed.
MACDUFF: What should he be?
MALCOLM: It is myself I mean, in whom I know
All the particulars of vice so grafted,
That, when they shall be opened, black Macbeth
Will seem as pure as snow, and the poor state
Esteem him as a lamb, being compared
With my confineless harms.
MACDUFF: Not in the legions
Of horrid hell can come a devil more damned
In evils to top Macbeth.
MALCOLM: I grant him bloody,
Luxurious, avaricious, false, deceitful,
Sudden, malicious, smacking of every sin
That has a name. But there's no bottom, none,
In my voluptuousness. Your wives, your daughters,
Your matrons, and your maids could not fill up
The cistern of my lust, and my desire

29. "It was perhaps your actions that made me suspicious of you."

32. *leave-taking* – saying goodbye

33 – 35. "Let not my suspicions and attempts to protect myself dishonour you."

37. *lay ... sure* – establish your foundation securely

39. *The ... affeered* – "Your right to the crown is legally confirmed."

41. *space* – realm

54. *more ... ways* – suffer more and in more ways

59. *opened* – disclosed (to view)

62. *confineless harms* – vices without limit

72. *cistern* – foul vessel or container

73. *All ... overbear* – would overcome all barriers to moderation

76 – 77. "Lack of control over one's appetites may be considered a usurpation of one's nature."

77. *It hath been* – It has caused

82. "And yet appear virtuous – the public may be deceived."

88. *ill-composed affection* – unbalanced disposition

89. *stanchless* – insatiable

90. *cut off* – kill

98. *summer-seeming* – hotter and short lasting (as is summer compared to the other seasons)

99. *sword* – cause of death

100. *foisons* – abundance

101. *mere own* – royal property belonging to you
portable – bearable

102. "When balanced out by your other graces or virtues."

108. *division* – variety

110. *concord* – harmony, peace

All continent impediments would overbear
That did oppose my will. Better Macbeth
Than such an one to reign.

Macduff: Boundless intemperance
In nature is a tyranny. It hath been
The untimely emptying of the happy throne,
And fall of many kings. But fear not yet
To take upon you what is yours. You may
Convey your pleasures in a spacious plenty
And yet seem cold — the time you may so hoodwink.
We have willing dames enough. There cannot be
That vulture in you to devour so many
As will to greatness dedicate themselves,
Finding it so inclined.

Malcolm: With this there grows
In my most ill-composed affection such
A stanchless avarice that, were I King,
I should cut off the nobles for their lands,
Desire his jewels and this other's house,
And my more-having would be as a sauce
To make me hunger more, that I should forge
Quarrels unjust against the good and loyal,
Destroying them for wealth.

Macduff: This avarice
Sticks deeper, grows with more pernicious root
Than summer-seeming lust, and it hath been
The sword of our slain kings. Yet do not fear.
Scotland hath foisons to fill up your will
Of your mere own. All these are portable,
With other graces weighed.

Malcolm: But I have none. The king-becoming graces,
As Justice, Verity, Temperance, Stableness,
Bounty, Perseverance, Mercy, Lowliness,
Devotion, Patience, Courage, Fortitude,
I have no relish of them, but abound
In the division of each several crime,
Acting it many ways. Nay, had I power, I should
Pour the sweet milk of concord into hell,
Uproar the universal peace, confound
All unity on earth.

Macduff: O Scotland! Scotland!

Malcolm: If such a one be fit to govern, speak.
I am as I have spoken.

Macduff: Fit to govern? No, not to live. O nation miserable!
With an untitled tyrant bloody-sceptered,

When shalt thou see thy wholesome days again,
Since that the truest issue of thy throne
By his own interdiction stands accursed
And does blaspheme his breed? Thy royal father
Was a most sainted King. The Queen that bore thee,
Oftener upon her knees than on her feet,
Died every day she lived. Fare thee well!
These evils thou repeatest upon thyself
Have banished me from Scotland. O my breast,
Thy hope ends here!

Malcolm: Macduff, this noble passion,
Child of integrity, hath from my soul
Wiped the black scruples, reconciled my thoughts
To thy good truth and honour. Devilish Macbeth
By many of these trains hath sought to win me
Into his power, and modest wisdom plucks me
From over-credulous haste. But God above
Deal between thee and me, for even now
I put myself to thy direction and
Unspeak mine own detraction, here abjure
The taints and blames I laid upon myself
For strangers to my nature. I am yet
Unknown to woman, never was forsworn,
Scarcely have coveted what was mine own,
At no time broke my faith, would not betray
The devil to his fellow, and delight
No less in truth than life. My first false speaking
Was this upon myself. What I am truly
Is thine and my poor country's to command.
Whither indeed, before thy here-approach,
Old Siward, with ten thousand warlike men
Already at a point, was setting forth.
Now we'll together, and the chance of goodness
Be like our warranted quarrel! Why are you silent?

Macduff: Such welcome and unwelcome things at once
'Tis hard to reconcile.

Enter a Doctor.

Malcolm: Well, more anon. Comes the King forth, I pray you?

Doctor: Ay, sir, there are a crew of wretched souls
That stay his cure. Their malady convinces
The great assay of art, but at his touch,
Such sanctity hath Heaven given his hand,
They presently amend.

119. *truest issue* – most legitimate heir
120. *interdiction* – prohibition; ban
124. *Died ... lived* – lived (devoutly) as if every day was her last
132. *trains* – plots
134. *over-credulous* – trusting and believing too easily (as did his father, Duncan)
137. *abjure* – retract
139. *For* – As being
140. *forsworn* – a breaker of oaths
141. *coveted* – desired; hungered for
147. *here-approach* – arrival
149. *at a point* – prepared for battle
151. *warranted quarrel* – just cause
156. *stay* – await
156. *convinces* – defeats
157. *great ... art* – best efforts of medical skill

162. *the evil* – "king's evil" or a form of tuberculosis.

163 – 175. It was believed that King Edward the Confessor was gifted with the power to heal through his touch. It was also believed that the gift became hereditary to succeeding English monarchs. The ability to cure by touch was seen as a sign of legitimacy to wear the crown. Both Queen Elizabeth I and King James I exercised this gift. This practice carried on well into the eighteenth century.

166. *visited* – afflicted

168. *mere* – complete, utter

169. *stamp* – gold coin (with the figure of St. Michael on it)

179. *betimes* – quickly

185. *Where nothing* – Where no one

188. *marked* – noticed

189. *modern ecstasy* – prevalent emotion

195 – 196. "Any report more than an hour old is hissed off the stage for being stale and out of date. Each minute gives birth to a new woe."

198. *well* – To the Elizabethans, "well" was a term used to not only describe the dead but also where they reside. Shakespeare often puns with this alternate connotation.

MALCOLM: I thank you, Doctor.

Exit Doctor.

MACDUFF: What's the disease he means?
MALCOLM: 'Tis called the Evil.
A most miraculous work in this good King,
Which often, since my here-remain in England,
I have seen him do. How he solicits heaven,
Himself best knows, but strangely-visited people,
All swollen and ulcerous, pitiful to the eye,
The mere despair of surgery, he cures,
Hanging a golden stamp about their necks,
Put on with holy prayers. And 'tis spoken,
To the succeeding royalty he leaves
The healing benediction. With this strange virtue
He hath a heavenly gift of prophecy,
And sundry blessings hang about his throne
That speak him full of grace.

Enter Ross.

MACDUFF: See, who comes here?
MALCOLM: My countryman, but yet I know him not.
MACDUFF: My ever gentle cousin, welcome hither.
MALCOLM: I know him now. Good God, betimes remove
The means that makes us strangers!
ROSS: Sir, amen.
MACDUFF: Stands Scotland where it did?
ROSS: Alas, poor country,
Almost afraid to know itself! It cannot
Be called our mother, but our grave. Where nothing,
But who knows nothing, is once seen to smile,
Where sighs and groans and shrieks that rend the air,
Are made, not marked, where violent sorrow seems
A modern ecstasy. The dead man's knell
Is there scarce asked for who, and good men's lives
Expire before the flowers in their caps,
Dying or ere they sicken.
MACDUFF: O, relation. Too nice, and yet too true!
MALCOLM: What's the newest grief?
ROSS: That of an hour's age doth hiss the speaker.
Each minute teems a new one.
MACDUFF: How does my wife?
ROSS: Why, well.

MACDUFF: And all my children?
ROSS: Well too.
MACDUFF: The tyrant has not battered at their peace?
ROSS: No, they were well at peace when I did leave them.
MACDUFF: Be not a niggard of your speech. How goest?
ROSS: When I came hither to transport the tidings,
Which I have heavily borne, there ran a rumour
Of many worthy fellows that were out,
Which was to my belief witnessed the rather,
For that I saw the tyrant's power afoot.
Now is the time of help. Your eye in Scotland
Would create soldiers, make our women fight,
To doff their dire distresses.
MALCOLM: Be it their comfort
We are coming thither. Gracious England hath
Lent us good Siward and ten thousand men.
An older and a better soldier none
That Christendom gives out.
ROSS: Would I could answer
This comfort with the like! But I have words
That would be howled out in the desert air,
Where hearing should not latch them.
MACDUFF: What concern they?
The general cause? Or is it a fee-grief
Due to some single breast?
ROSS: No mind that's honest
But in it shares some woe, though the main part
Pertains to you alone.
MACDUFF: If it be mine,
Keep it not from me. Quickly let me have it.
ROSS: Let not your ears despise my tongue for ever,
Which shall possess them with the heaviest sound
That ever yet they heard.
MACDUFF: Humh! I guess at it.
ROSS: Your castle is surprised, your wife and babes
Savagely slaughtered. To relate the manner
Were, on the quarry of these murdered deer,
To add the death of you.
MALCOLM: Merciful heaven!
What, man! Never pull your hat upon your brows.
Give sorrow words. The grief that does not speak
Whispers the overfraught heart, and bids it break.
MACDUFF: My children too?
ROSS: Wife, children, servants, all that could be found.
MACDUFF: And I must be from thence! My wife killed too?

203. *niggard* – stingy
206. *were out* – in open revolt against (Macbeth)
207. *to ... witnessed* – confirmed what I had already thought
209. *of* – for

soldiers' camp

220. *latch* – catch
222. *fee-grief* – private sorrow

235. *quarry* – pile of bodies (usually of game killed during a hunt)
238. "What, man! Do not cover your face."
240. *overfraught* – overburdened

Ross: I have said.
Malcolm: Be comforted.
Let's make us medicines of our great revenge,
To cure this deadly grief.
Macduff: He has no children. — All my pretty ones?
Did you say all? O Hell-kite! All?
What, all my pretty chickens and their dam
At one fell swoop?
Malcolm: Dispute it like a man.
Macduff: I shall do so,
But I must also feel it as a man.
I cannot but remember such things were
That were most precious to me. Did heaven look on,
And would not take their part? Sinful Macduff,
They were all struck for thee! Naught that I am,
Not for their own demerits, but for mine,
Fell slaughter on their souls. Heaven rest them now!
Malcolm: Be this the whetstone of your sword. Let grief
Convert to anger. Blunt not the heart, enrage it.
Macduff: O, I could play the woman with mine eyes
And braggart with my tongue! But, gentle Heavens,
Cut short all intermission. Front to front
Bring thou this fiend of Scotland and myself.
Within my sword's length set him. If he 'scape,
Heaven forgive him too!
Malcolm: This tune goes manly.
Come, go we to the King. Our power is ready,
Our lack is nothing but our leave. Macbeth
Is ripe for shaking, and the Powers above
Put on their instruments. Receive what cheer you may,
The night is long that never finds the day.

Exeunt.

260. *fell* – cruel

265. *intermission* – delay

271. *Our ... leave.* "All that is left to do is to say goodbye."

273. *Put ... instruments* – arm themselves

Act Four Considerations

ACT FOUR Scene 1

- Discuss the irony of the witches' statement that "Something wicked this way comes."
- What further evidence is there in this scene that Macbeth has become totally wicked?
- The ingredients of the witches' cauldron consist of what was considered vile and repugnant during the Elizabethan period. Write a parody of their speech. Include ingredients that a modern-day audience would find equally disgusting.
- Summarize the three prophecies that the apparitions give Macbeth. How does he react to them? What does this reveal about Macbeth's state of mind? How does he react to the show of eight kings?

ACT FOUR Scene 2

- Do you think Macduff was justified in leaving his family in Scotland? Respond to this question by writing a letter, either from Macduff to his wife explaining his decision, or from Lady Macduff to her husband expressing her opinion of the decision.
- What dramatic purpose is served by the short scene between Lady Macduff and her son?
- In what significant ways does the murder of Macduff's family differ from Macbeth's previous crimes?

ACT FOUR Scene 3

- How does Malcolm test Macduff's loyalty? This action of Malcolm's serves to contrast him with his father. How so? What other comparisons can be made between Malcolm and Duncan?
- It is unclear as to whom Macduff's comment "He has no children" (line 248) refers. What arguments can be offered to justify the opinion that it refers to Macbeth? to Malcolm?
- What lines in the scene reinforce the notion that Macduff will be Macbeth's nemesis?

Act Five

Scene 1

Dunsinane.

A room in the castle.

Enter a Doctor of Physic and a Waiting Gentlewoman.

DOCTOR: I have two nights watched with you, but can perceive no truth in your report. When was it she last walked?

GENTLEWOMAN: Since his Majesty went into the field, I have seen her rise from her bed, throw her nightgown upon her, unlock her closet, take forth paper, fold it, write upon it, read it, afterwards seal it, and again return to bed. Yet all this while in a most fast sleep.

DOCTOR: A great perturbation in nature, to receive at once the benefit of sleep and do the effects of watching! In this slumbery agitation, besides her walking and other actual performances, what, at any time, have you heard her say?

GENTLEWOMAN: That, sir, which I will not report after her.

DOCTOR: You may to me, and 'tis most meet you should.

GENTLEWOMAN: Neither to you nor anyone, having no witness to confirm my speech.

Enter Lady Macbeth with a taper.

Lo you, here she comes! This is her very guise, and, upon my life, fast asleep. Observe her. Stand close.

DOCTOR: How came she by that light?

GENTLEWOMAN: Why, it stood by her. She has light by her continually. 'Tis her command.

DOCTOR: You see, her eyes are open.

GENTLEWOMAN: Ay, but their sense are shut.

Lady Macbeth has been observed sleep-walking and talking for several nights. A Doctor has been summoned by her attendant to observe her nightly ritual. Lady Macbeth appears, and in her sleep-walking state she relives details of the murders for which she and Macbeth have been responsible. Both the Doctor and the Gentlewoman are shocked by what they witness. The Doctor realizes there is nothing he can do to help and advises that a careful watch be placed on Lady Macbeth.

8. *perturbation* – disturbance; disorder

13. *meet* – appropriate; proper

28. *set* – write

38. *starting* – nervous behaviour; flinching

46. *sorely charged* – painfully afflicted

48. *dignity* – rank; social status

DOCTOR: What is it she does now? Look how she rubs her hands.

GENTLEWOMAN: It is an accustomed action with her, to seem thus washing her hands. I have known her continue in this a quarter of an hour.

LADY MACBETH: Yet here's a spot.

DOCTOR: Hark, she speaks! I will set down what comes from her, to satisfy my remembrance the more strongly.

LADY MACBETH: Out, damned spot! Out, I say! One - two - why then 'tis time to do it. Hell is murky. Fie, my lord, fie! A soldier, and afeard? What need we fear who knows it, when none can call our power to account? Yet who would have thought the old man to have had so much blood in him?

DOCTOR: Do you mark that?

LADY MACBETH: The Thane of Fife had a wife. Where is she now? What, will these hands never be clean? No more of that, my lord, no more of that. You mar all with this starting.

DOCTOR: Go to, go to.
You have known what you should not.

GENTLEWOMAN: She has spoke what she should not,
I am sure of that. Heaven knows what she has known.

LADY MACBETH: Here's the smell of the blood still.
All the perfumes of Arabia will not sweeten this little hand.
Oh, oh, oh!

DOCTOR: What a sigh is there! The heart is sorely charged.

GENTLEWOMAN: I would not have such a heart in my bosom for the dignity of the whole body.

DOCTOR: Well, well, well.

GENTLEWOMAN: Pray God it be, sir.

DOCTOR: This disease is beyond my practice. Yet I have known those which have walked in their sleep who have died holily in their beds.

LADY MACBETH: Wash your hands, put on your nightgown, look not so pale. I tell you yet again, Banquo's buried. He cannot come out on his grave.

DOCTOR: Even so?

LADY MACBETH: To bed, to bed. There's knocking at the gate. Come, come, come, come, give me your hand. What's done cannot be undone. To bed, to bed, to bed.

Exit.

DOCTOR: Will she go now to bed?

GENTLEWOMAN: Directly.

DOCTOR: Foul whisperings are abroad. Unnatural deeds
Do breed unnatural troubles. Infected minds
To their deaf pillows will discharge their secrets.
More needs she the divine than the physician.
God, God, forgive us all! Look after her.
Remove from her the means of all annoyance,
And still keep eyes upon her. So good night.
My mind she has mated and amazed my sight.
I think, but dare not speak.
GENTLEWOMAN: Good night, good Doctor.

Exeunt.

63 – 64. *Unnatural ... troubles* – actions that violate the natural order of the universe. See note Act Two Scene 4, line 12.
64. *Infected minds* – Guilt-filled hearts
66. *divine* – priest
70. *mated* – bewildered

A Scottish army is on its way towards Birnam Wood to join up with the English forces led by Malcolm and Siward. Angus expresses the view that those few who continue to serve Macbeth do so not out of loyalty or love but only out of fear.

colours

4. *alarm* – call to arms
5. *mortified* – dead

9. *file* – list

11. *unrough* – beardless; young
12. *protest* – proclaim

17 – 18. "Just as a diseased and bloated man cannot buckle his belt, so Macbeth cannot maintain control of his country."

21. "Now, minute by minute, there are new revolts to protest his treachery."

Act Five
Scene 2

The countryside near Dunsinane.

Drum and colours. Enter Menteith, Caithness, Angus, Lennox, and Soldiers.

MENTEITH: The English power is near, led on by Malcolm,
His uncle Siward, and the good Macduff.
Revenges burn in them, for their dear causes
Would to the bleeding and the grim alarm
Excite the mortified man.
ANGUS: Near Birnam Wood
Shall we well meet them. That way are they coming.
CAITHNESS: Who knows if Donalbain be with his brother?
LENNOX: For certain, sir, he is not; I have a file
Of all the gentry. There is Siward's son
And many unrough youths that even now
Protest their first of manhood.
MENTEITH: What does the tyrant?
CAITHNESS: Great Dunsinane he strongly fortifies.
Some say he's mad. Others, that lesser hate him,
Do call it valiant fury. But, for certain,
He cannot buckle his distempered cause
Within the belt of rule.
ANGUS: Now does he feel
His secret murders sticking on his hands,
Now minutely revolts upbraid his faith-breach.
Those he commands move only in command,
Nothing in love. Now does he feel his title
Hang loose about him, like a giant's robe
Upon a dwarfish thief.

MENTEITH: Who then shall blame
His pestered senses to recoil and start,
When all that is within him does condemn
Itself for being there?
CAITHNESS: Well, march we on
To give obedience where 'tis truly owed.
Meet we the medicine of the sickly weal,
And with him pour we, in our country's purge,
Each drop of us.
LENNOX: Or so much as it needs
To dew the sovereign flower and drown the weeds.
Make we our march towards Birnam.

Exeunt marching.

27. *pestered senses* – troubled mind

32. *sickly weal* – sick country
33. "And with him, we dedicate ourselves to the cleansing of our country."
36. *dew* – water
36. *sovereign flower* – all-powerful healing king. Malcolm is the medicinal herb that will cure Scotland.

Act Five

Scene 3

Dunsinane.

Reports that the nobles are deserting him do not bother Macbeth. Because of the prophecies, Macbeth remains confident that he cannot be defeated. He receives a report that ten thousand English soldiers are approaching his castle. As he puts on his battle garb, Macbeth discusses the Queen's condition with the Doctor.

3. *taint* – be infected; become weak

8. *epicures* – those with refined eating tastes. Macbeth means this as an insult. The English are being referred to as fussy weaklings who are preoccupied with sampling fine foods and not with matters of war.

9. *sway* – rule

16. "Pinch your pale and fearful cheeks till they turn red"

17. *patch* – fool

19. *Are ... fear* – will counsel (persuade) others to be fearful

23. *push* – attack; challenge

26. *sere* – dried state; withered

A room in the castle.
Enter Macbeth, Doctor, and Attendants.

Macbeth: Bring me no more reports. Let them fly all!
Till Birnam Wood remove to Dunsinane,
I cannot taint with fear. What's the boy Malcolm?
Was he not born of woman? The spirits that know
All mortal consequences have pronounced me thus:
"Fear not, Macbeth: No man that's born of woman
Shall ever have power upon thee." Then fly, false Thanes,
And mingle with the English epicures!
The mind I sway by and the heart I bear
Shall never sag with doubt nor shake with fear.

Enter a Servant.

The devil damn thee black, thou cream-faced loon!
Where gottest thou that goose look?
Servant: There is ten thousand —
Macbeth: Geese, villain?
Servant: Soldiers, sir.
Macbeth: Go prick thy face and over-red thy fear,
Thou lily-livered boy. What soldiers, patch?
Death of thy soul! Those linen cheeks of thine
Are counsellors to fear. What soldiers, whey-face?
Servant: The English force, so please you.
Macbeth: Take thy face hence.

Exit Servant.

Seyton! — I am sick at heart,
When I behold — Seyton, I say! — This push
Will cheer me ever or disseat me now.
I have lived long enough. My way of life
Is fallen into the sere, the yellow leaf,
And that which should accompany old age,

As honour, love, obedience, troops of friends,
I must not look to have. But in their stead,
Curses, not loud but deep, mouth-honour, breath,
Which the poor heart would fain deny and dare not.
Seyton!

Enter Seyton.

SEYTON: What's your gracious pleasure?
MACBETH: What news more?
SEYTON: All is confirmed, my lord, which was reported.
MACBETH: I'll fight, till from my bones my flesh be hacked.
Give me my armour.
SEYTON: 'Tis not needed yet.
MACBETH: I'll put it on.
Send out more horses, skirr the country round.
Hang those that talk of fear. Give me mine armour.
How does your patient, Doctor?
DOCTOR: Not so sick, my lord,
As she is troubled with thick-coming fancies,
That keep her from her rest.
MACBETH: Cure her of that.
Canst thou not minister to a mind diseased,
Pluck from the memory a rooted sorrow,
Raze out the written troubles of the brain,
And with some sweet oblivious antidote
Cleanse the stuffed bosom of that perilous stuff
Which weighs upon the heart?
DOCTOR: Therein the patient
Must minister to himself.
MACBETH: Throw physic to the dogs, I'll none of it.
Come, put mine armour on. Give me my staff.
Seyton, send out. — Doctor, the Thanes fly from me. —
Come, sir, dispatch. — If thou couldst, doctor, cast
The water of my land, find her disease
And purge it to a sound and pristine health,
I would applaud thee to the very echo,
That should applaud again. — Pull it off, I say. —
What rhubarb, senna, or what purgative drug
Would scour these English hence? Hearest thou of them?
DOCTOR: Ay, my good lord, your royal preparation
Makes us hear something.
MACBETH: Bring it after me. —
I will not be afraid of death and bane
Till Birnam Forest come to Dunsinane.
DOCTOR: *[Aside.]* Were I from Dunsinane away and clear,
Profit again should hardly draw me here.

Exeunt.

30. *mouth-honour, breath* – honour paid with insincere words
31. *fain deny* – wish to retract
40. *skirr* – scour
44. *thick-coming fancies* – numerous hallucinations
50. *oblivious* – that which causes forgetfulness
51. *stuffed bosom* – heart filled with grief
55. *physic* – medical science
58. *cast* – analyze (as in urine samples)
61 – 62. "I would clap till the echo of my clapping joins in the applause."
63. *rhubarb, senna* – plants used as laxatives
68. *bane* – destruction
71. *draw me here* – bring me back

On their way to Macbeth's castle, Malcolm and the English forces stop at Birnam Wood. Malcolm orders the soldiers to cut branches from the trees to use as camouflage during their march towards Macbeth's castle.

Act Five

Scene 4

Country near Birnam Wood.

Drum and colours. Enter Malcolm, Siward, Macduff, Siward's Son, Menteith, Caithness, Angus, Lennox, Ross, and Soldiers, marching.

MALCOLM: Cousins, I hope the days are near at hand
That chambers will be safe.
MENTEITH: We doubt it nothing.
SIWARD: What wood is this before us?
MENTEITH: The wood of Birnam.

2. "That we can sleep at night without fear of being murdered in our beds."

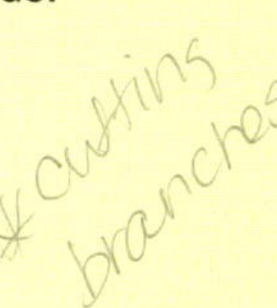

MALCOLM: Let every soldier hew him down a bough,
And bear it before him. Thereby shall we shadow
The numbers of our host and make discovery
Err in report of us.
SOLDIERS: It shall be done.
SIWARD: We learn no other but the confident tyrant
Keeps still in Dunsinane and will endure
Our setting down before it.
MALCOLM: 'Tis his main hope;
For where there is advantage to be gone,
Both more and less have given him the revolt,
And none serve with him but constrained things
Whose hearts are absent too.
MACDUFF: Let our just censures
Attend the true event, and put we on
Industrious soldiership.
SIWARD: The time approaches
That will with due decision make us know
What we shall say we have and what we owe.
Thoughts speculative, their unsure hopes relate,
But certain issue, strokes must arbitrate.
Towards which, advance the war.

Exeunt marching.

8. *discovery* – scouts' reports

12. *endure* – allow
15. *advantage to be gone* – opportunity to leave
16. *more and less* – the noble-born and commoners
17. *constrained things* – weaklings
19 – 21. "Let's not waste time talking about the defectors from Macbeth's camp until the end of the campaign, and let's instead apply ourselves to the battle ahead."
25. "Speculations serve only to raise false hopes."
26. "Fighting will determine the final (and certain) outcome."
27. *advance* – let us go forward to

Macbeth feels secure behind the mighty battlements of his castle. He hears the cry of women and is informed that his wife is dead. This sparks in him thoughts about the meaninglessness of life. New reports claim that Birnam Wood is marching towards Dunsinane.

Act Five
Scene 5

Dunsinane.

Within the castle.

Enter Macbeth, Seyton, and Soldiers, with drum and colours.

MACBETH: Hang out our banners on the outward walls.
The cry is still, "They come!" Our castle's strength
Will laugh a siege to scorn. Here let them lie
Till famine and the ague eat them up.
Were they not forced with those that should be ours,
We might have met them dareful, beard to beard,
And beat them backward home.

A cry within of women.

What is that noise?
SEYTON: It is the cry of women, my good lord.

Exit.

MACBETH: I have almost forgot the taste of fears.
The time has been, my senses would have cooled
To hear a night-shriek, and my fell of hair
Would at a dismal treatise rouse and stir
As life were in it. I have supped full with horrors.
Direness, familiar to my slaughterous thoughts,
Cannot once start me.

[Enter Seyton.]

Wherefore was that cry?
SEYTON: The Queen, my lord, is dead.

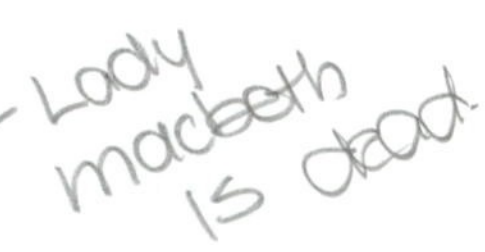

4. *ague* – chills, fevers
5. *forced* – reinforced
6. *dareful* – openly; boldly

12. *fell* – skin with hair on it
13. "Would stand on end"
15. *Direness* – horrors
16. *start* – move; affect

19 – 20. *She ... word* – The intention of these two lines is much disputed. Some argue that Macbeth means that she died before her time and that she should have died later in the future. Others maintain that Macbeth regrets that he does not have time to grieve for her because he is too busy preparing for his confrontation with the attacking forces.

MACBETH: She should have died hereafter.
There would have been a time for such a word. —
Tomorrow, and tomorrow, and tomorrow
Creeps in this petty pace from day to day
To the last syllable of recorded time,
And all our yesterdays have lighted fools
The way to dusty death. Out, out, brief candle!
Life's but a walking shadow, a poor player,
That struts and frets his hour upon the stage
And then is heard no more. It is a tale
Told by an idiot, full of sound and fury,
Signifying nothing.

Enter a Messenger.

Thou comest to use thy tongue. Thy story quickly.
MESSENGER: Gracious my lord,
I should report that which I say I saw,
But know not how to do it.
MACBETH: Well, say, sir.
MESSENGER: As I did stand my watch upon the hill,
I looked toward Birnam, and anon, methought,
The Wood began to move.
MACBETH: Liar and slave!
MESSENGER: Let me endure your wrath, if it be not so.
Within this three mile may you see it coming.
I say, a moving grove.
MACBETH: If thou speakest false,
Upon the next tree shalt thou hang alive,
Till famine cling thee. If thy speech be sooth,
I care not if thou dost for me as much.
I pull in resolution and begin
To doubt the equivocation of the fiend
That lies like truth. "Fear not, till Birnam Wood
Do come to Dunsinane," and now a wood
Comes toward Dunsinane. — Arm, arm, and out! —
If this which he avouches does appear,
There is nor flying hence nor tarrying here.
I begin to be aweary of the sun
And wish the estate of the world were now undone. —
Ring the alarum bell! Blow, wind! Come, wrack!
At least we'll die with harness on our back.

Exeunt.

25. *dusty death* – "For dust thou art and unto dust thou shalt return." (Genesis 3.19)
25. *brief candle* – short life

RELATED READING

"Out, Out —" – poem by Robert Frost (page 142)

26. *shadow* – Actors were frequently referred to as "shadows."

"Life is not a 'brief candle.' It is a splendid torch that I want to make burn as brightly as possible before handing it on to future generations."
– George Bernard Shaw (1856 – 1950) English playwright and essayist

40. *endure* – suffer

45. *sooth* – true

47. "My resolution begins to falter"

53. *tarrying* – remaining
55. *estate of the world* – order of the universe. He wishes the world would end.

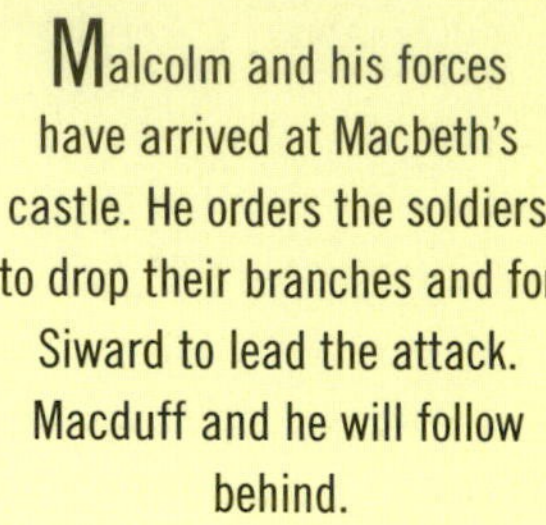

Malcolm and his forces have arrived at Macbeth's castle. He orders the soldiers to drop their branches and for Siward to lead the attack. Macduff and he will follow behind.

Act Five

Scene 6

The Same.

A plain before the castle.

Drum and colours. Enter Malcolm, Siward, Macduff, and their Army, with boughs.

MALCOLM: Now, near enough.
Your leavy screens throw down
And show like those you are. You, worthy uncle,
Shall with my cousin, your right noble son,
Lead our first battle. Worthy Macduff and we
Shall take upon us what else remains to do,
According to our order.
SIWARD: Fare you well.
Do we but find the tyrant's power tonight,
Let us be beaten if we cannot fight.
MACDUFF: Make all our trumpets speak. Give them all breath,
Those clamorous harbingers of blood and death.

Exeunt. Alarums continue.

7. *order* – plan

9. *Do we but ...* – If only we

12. *clamorous harbingers* – noisy forerunners

"A burning would is come to dance inane"
– James Joyce (1882 – 1941) Irish novelist and short story writer

Act Five
Scene 7

Dunsinane.

Before the castle.

Enter Macbeth.

Macbeth: They have tied me to a stake. I cannot fly,
But bear-like, I must fight the course. What's he
That was not born of woman? Such a one
Am I to fear, or none.

Enter young Siward.

Young Siward: What is thy name?
Macbeth: Thou'lt be afraid to hear it.
Young Siward: No, though thou callest thyself a hotter name
Than any is in hell.
Macbeth: My name's Macbeth.
Young Siward: The devil himself could not pronounce a title
More hateful to mine ear.
Macbeth: No, nor more fearful.
Young Siward: Thou liest, abhorred tyrant. With my sword
I'll prove the lie thou speakest.

They fight, and young Siward is slain.

Macbeth: Thou wast born of woman.—
But swords I smile at, weapons laugh to scorn,
Brandished by man that's of a woman born.

Exit. Alarums. Enter Macduff.

A confident Macbeth abandons the security of the castle and challenges all comers on the battlefield. He finds himself cornered with no means of escape. But Macbeth is still confident that the second prediction ("no one of woman born shall harm Macbeth") will protect him. Young Siward comes upon Macbeth and is killed by him. Macduff appears seeking Macbeth out. Siward announces that the castle has surrendered and that the battle will soon be over.

2. *bear-like* – a reference to the Elizabethan sport of bear-baiting, in which a bear is chained to a stake and dogs are set upon it

bear-baiting

MACDUFF: That way the noise is. Tyrant, show thy face!
If thou be'st slain and with no stroke of mine,
My wife and children's ghosts will haunt me still.
I cannot strike at wretched Kerns, whose arms
Are hired to bear their staves. Either thou, Macbeth,
Or else my sword, with an unbattered edge,
I sheathe again undeeded. There thou shouldst be.
By this great clatter, one of greatest note
Seems bruited. Let me find him, Fortune!
And more I beg not.

Exit. Alarums.
Enter Malcolm and old Siward.

SIWARD: This way, my lord. The castle's gently rendered.
The tyrant's people on both sides do fight.
The noble Thanes do bravely in the war.
The day almost itself professes yours
And little is to do.
MALCOLM: We have met with foes
That strike beside us.
SIWARD: Enter, sir, the castle.

Exeunt. Alarum.

21 – 22. "I cannot strike at lowly foot–soldiers who are but mercenaries paid to bear arms."
24. *undeeded* – unused

26. *bruited* – announced

28. *rendered* – surrendered

34. *strike beside us* – perhaps this means "intentionally avoid striking me"

RELATED READING

Macbeth – poem by Stuart Dischell *(page 148)*

Act Five

Scene 8

Another part of the field.

Enter Macbeth.

Macbeth: Why should I play the Roman fool and die
On mine own sword? Whiles I see lives, the gashes
Do better upon them.

Enter Macduff.

Macduff: Turn, Hell-hound, turn!
Macbeth: Of all men else I have avoided thee.
But get thee back, my soul is too much charged
With blood of thine already.
Macduff: I have no words.
My voice is in my sword, thou bloodier villain
Than terms can give thee out!

They fight. Alarum.

Macbeth: Thou losest labour.
As easy mayst thou the intrenchant air
With thy keen sword impress as make me bleed.
Let fall thy blade on vulnerable crests.
I bear a charmed life, which must not yield
To one of woman born.
Macduff: Despair thy charm,
And let the Angel whom thou still hast served
Tell thee, Macduff was from his mother's womb
Untimely ripped.
Macbeth: Accursed be that tongue that tells me so,
For it hath cowed my better part of man.
And be these juggling fiends no more believed,

Macduff and Macbeth fight. At first, Macduff does poorly against Macbeth, who brags about his charmed life. Macduff reveals that he was "untimely ripped" from his mother's womb. Macbeth is so shocked that at first he refuses to fight with Macduff. Macduff kills Macbeth and drags him off. Malcolm and Siward arrive and they learn that Siward's son has been killed. Macduff reappears carrying Macbeth's head. Malcolm is hailed King and he promises to restore order and peace to the nation.

1. *Roman fool* – Rather than suffer capture and humiliation at the hands of their enemies, some high-ranking Roman officers chose to commit suicide.

6. *too much charged* – too full of guilt
10. "Than words can describe."
11. "You are wasting your breath."
12. *intrenchant* – unable to be cut
20. *untimely ripped* – Caesarian birth. This would not be considered being born naturally from woman.
22. *cowed* – made a coward of
23. *juggling* – deceiving (they juggle the truth)

24. *palter* – equivocate; trifle

29. *monsters* – freaks (in a sideshow)

30. Macbeth's picture would be painted and hung on a pole with words describing his crimes to accompany it.

47. *unshrinking station* – post he did not give up

53. *Had ... before?* – The answer to this question is important for Siward. If his son's wounds were on his back, this would mean he died fleeing from the battle. If his wounds were on the front, this would mean that he had died a soldier's death.

That palter with us in a double sense,
That keep the word of promise to our ear
And break it to our hope! I'll not fight with thee.

MACDUFF: Then yield thee, coward,
And live to be the show and gaze of the time.
We'll have thee, as our rarer monsters are,
Painted upon a pole, and underwrit,
"Here may you see the tyrant."

MACBETH: I will not yield,
To kiss the ground before young Malcolm's feet
And to be baited with the rabble's curse.
Though Birnam Wood be come to Dunsinane,
And thou opposed, being of no woman born,
Yet I will try the last. Before my body
I throw my warlike shield! Lay on, Macduff,
And damned be him that first cries, "Hold, enough!"

Exeunt fighting. Alarums.
They re-enter fighting, and Macbeth is slain.
[Macduff exits dragging off Macbeth's body.]
Retreat and Flourish. Enter, with drum and colours, Malcolm, Siward, Ross, Thanes, and Soldiers.

MALCOLM: I would the friends we miss were safe arrived.

SIWARD: Some must go off, and yet, by these I see,
So great a day as this is cheaply bought.

MALCOLM: Macduff is missing, and your noble son.

ROSS: Your son, my lord, has paid a soldier's debt.
He only lived but till he was a man,
The which no sooner had his prowess confirmed
In the unshrinking station where he fought
But like a man he died.

SIWARD: Then he is dead?

ROSS: Ay, and brought off the field. Your cause of sorrow
Must not be measured by his worth, for then
It hath no end.

SIWARD: Had he his hurts before?

ROSS: Ay, on the front.

SIWARD: Why then, God's soldier be he!
Had I as many sons as I have hairs,
I would not wish them to a fairer death.
And so his knell is knolled.

MALCOLM: He's worth more sorrow,
And that I'll spend for him.

SIWARD: He's worth no more.

They say he parted well and paid his score,
And so God be with him! Here comes newer comfort.

Enter Macduff, with Macbeth's head.

MACDUFF: Hail, King, for so thou art.
Behold where stands
The usurper's cursed head. The time is free.
I see thee compassed with thy kingdom's pearl
That speak my salutation in their minds,
Whose voices I desire aloud with mine —
Hail, King of Scotland!
ALL: Hail, King of Scotland!

Flourish.

MALCOLM: We shall not spend a large expense of time
Before we reckon with your several loves
And make us even with you. My Thanes and kinsmen,
Henceforth be Earls, the first that ever Scotland
In such an honour named. What's more to do,
Which would be planted newly with the time —
As calling home our exiled friends abroad
That fled the snares of watchful tyranny,
Producing forth the cruel ministers
Of this dead butcher and his fiend-like Queen,
Who, as 'tis thought, by self and violent hands
Took off her life — this, and what needful else
That calls upon us, by the grace of Grace
We will perform in measure, time, and place.
So thanks to all at once and to each one,
Whom we invite to see us crowned at Scone.

Flourish. Exeunt.

FINIS

62. *score* – debt

66. *time is free* – liberty has been restored
67. *compassed* – surrounded
67. *pearl* – nobles

"*Macbeth* is a tale told by a genius, full of soundness and fury, signifying many things."
– James Thurber (1894 – 1961), American humorist

73. *reckon* – reward

80. "Force out of hiding Macbeth's agents and accomplices."

84. *Grace* – God

Act Five Considerations

ACT FIVE Scene 1

- Why is the Gentlewoman reluctant to repeat what she has heard the sleep-walking Lady Macbeth say?
- What is ironic about Lady Macbeth's state of mind? What lines from previous scenes prepare us for this change in Lady Macbeth?
- Imagine you are the Doctor and have just finished examining Lady Macbeth. Write a medical report in which you make a diagnosis and provide a rationale for the instructions you have given the Gentlewoman about Lady Macbeth's care.

ACT FIVE Scene 2

- Read Caroline Spurgeon's essay on "The Imagery of *Macbeth*" on page 123. What major categories of images does she argue pervade the play? What examples of these images occur in this scene?
- What dramatic purposes are served by this scene? What information is revealed concerning the forces amassing against Macbeth?

ACT FIVE Scene 3

- How does Macbeth feel when he hears of the flight of the Thanes? What emotions are expressed in his speech beginning line 22, "I am sick at heart. . ."?
- Macbeth changes his mind about putting on his armour. What does this reveal about his mental state?
- With what tone of voice do you think Macbeth would speak to the Doctor at the end of the scene? Why?

ACT FIVE Scene 4

- Why is it appropriate that Malcolm give the order to cut down trees for use as camouflage?
- Imagine you are a newspaper or television reporter. Write a short report summarizing the events in this scene.

ACT FIVE Scene 5

- Macbeth expresses confidence about surviving a siege. If you were his military advisor, what advice would you give him?

- In Macbeth's "Tomorrow, and tomorrow ..." soliloquy, he uses a theatrical metaphor to express his disillusionment with life. Rewrite the speech using a different metaphor. For example, you could choose a sports or politics or school metaphor.

- What is Macbeth's mood at the end of the scene? By this point in the play, what different emotions could the audience be feeling for Macbeth?

ACT FIVE Scene 6

- If you were a director of a modern, high-tech version of the play, how would you emphasize Macduff's eagerness to fight Macbeth? Be creative.

ACT FIVE Scene 7

- What dramatic purpose is served by having Macbeth fight and kill Young Siward?

ACT FIVE Scene 8

- What do you think of Siward's response upon hearing the news of his son's death? Write a dialogue in which Siward tells his wife of their son's fate.

- What kingly qualities does Malcolm display in his last speech?

The 10 Most Difficult Questions One Can Ask about *Macbeth*

Shakespeare's works have survived for over 400 years. Is it because of his great stories and characters? Perhaps, but this would also be true of several of his contemporaries, and they haven't fared as well as Shakespeare. There must be something else. Perhaps one reason is his ambiguity. It is ironic that Shakespeare's most frustrating quality could very well be his greatest strength. His classic lines, his unforgettable characters, and his "problem" plays can be interpreted in many different ways. There are so many unanswered and unanswerable questions in the plays that generations of readers and critics to come will continue to ask questions and pore over his works for as long as literature and poetry are valued.

Macbeth is no exception when it comes to difficult questions. Here are just a few of them to challenge your thinking about the play. You are invited to choose one or more for a closer focus and study. The end result of your efforts may take the form of a research essay or a position paper. To attempt to answer these questions you will need to probe the text carefully and consult secondary sources. You must also be prepared to take a stand.

Once you have chosen a question to focus on, you will need to do the following:

- present as effective an argument as you can for the conventional or most straightforward interpretation;
- discuss fully the problems with this interpretation; and
- offer and justify your own interpretation with evidence from the text and/or secondary reading materials.

Here are 10 of the most difficult questions about the play Macbeth:

1. Who is Bellona's bridegroom: Macbeth or Macduff? What evidence is there that Macbeth did not participate in the battle at Fife? Try to build a case for Macduff as Bellona's bridegroom.

2. Are the Three Sisters witches, or are they merely instruments of fate—weyard sisters? What is gained if we do not think of the Three Sisters as witches? What is lost?

3. Are the floating dagger and Banquo's ghost creations of Macbeth's imagination or are they real? Which view makes for better drama?

4. Who is most responsible for the bloodshed that occurs in the play? Is it Macbeth alone or is Lady Macbeth to blame? How much blame can we place on the "instruments of darkness"?

5. In what significant ways does Shakespeare's Macbeth differ from the historical figure as presented in *Holinshed's Chronicles*? Why does Shakespeare make such dramatic changes from the historical record?

6. Did Shakespeare write the Hecate scene (Act Three, scene 5)? Many scholars agree that he did not. Some think he did. What do you think?

7. When Macbeth hears that his wife is dead, he states that "She should have died hereafter. There would have been time for such a word." What does he mean by this?

8. According to *Holinshed's Chronicles*, Banquo was an accessory to Duncan's murder. Shakespeare changes this in his treatment of the story. Some scholars believe that Shakespeare paints a positive portrait of Banquo as a compliment to King James. Others disagree. Is Banquo presented as a positive character in the play? Would James be flattered by this kind of portrayal of his ancestor?

9. Is Macbeth a tragic hero according to the classical definition of the term or is he merely a monster? Does Shakespeare succeed in creating sympathy for Macbeth?

10. What basis is there for believing in the curse of the Scottish play?

Macbeth *and the* Witches

by Richard Armour

The story of Macbeth like you have never heard it before. For Richard Armour, nothing is sacred – including the Bard!

Three witches, extremely weird sisters, are having a picnic amidst thunder and lightning somewhere in Scotland. Judging from their appearance, they placed one-two-three in the Edinburgh Ugly Contest. "When shall we three meet again in thunder, lightning, or in rain?" asks one of them. They hate nice weather and are happiest when they are soaking wet and their hair is all stringy.

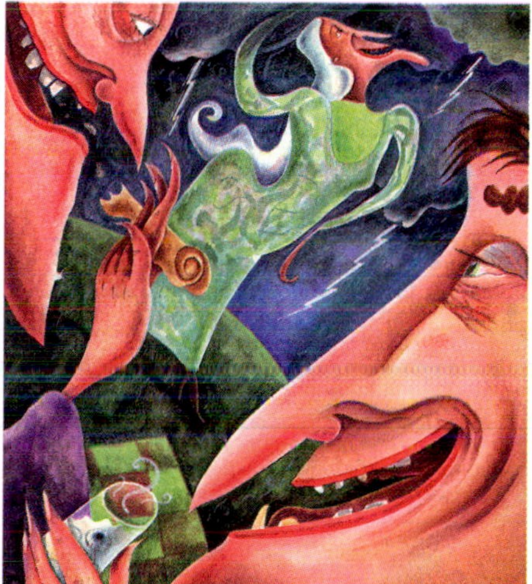

"When the hurly-burly's done,[1] when the battle's lost and won," another replies. A battle is going on between the forces of Duncan, the King of Scotland, and some Norwegians, assisted by the rebel Thane of Cawdor. At the moment it's looking good for Duncan, because two of his generals, Macbeth and Banquo, have cunningly put bagpipes into the hands of the enemy, who are blowing their brains out.

The witches hear some dear friends[2] calling, and depart. "Fair is foul, and foul is fair," they comment philosophically as they leave. This must have been pretty upsetting to any moralists, semanticists, or baseball umpires who chanced to overhear them. Shortly afterward, the battle having been won by Macbeth, and the weather having turned bad enough to be pleasant, the witches meet again.

"Where hast thou been, Sister?" asks one.

"Killing swine," the second replies. All three of them have been busy doing similarly diverting things, and one of them happily shows the others the thumb of a drowned sailor which she is adding to her thumb collection.[3]

---

1. See also hurdy-gurdy, hunky-dory, and okey-dokey.
2. A cat and a toad. Witches have to make friendships where they can.
3. In a comedy, this would be considered tragic relief.

Macbeth and Banquo come by at this point, on their way to inform the King that they have defeated the rebels. They would rather tell him in person than render a report in triplicate.

"Speak, if you can," says Macbeth boldly to the hags. "What are you?" He rather thinks they are witches, but would like to hear it from their own skinny lips.

The witches start hailing.[4] They hail Macbeth as Thane of Glamis and Thane of Cawdor and say he will be King Hereafter. Not to leave Banquo out, they hail him as "lesser than Macbeth, and greater." (The witches are masters of gobbledyspook.) He won't be a king, they say, but he'll beget kings, and now they have to begetting along.

Not to leave Banquo out, they hail him as "lesser than Macbeth, and greater." (The witches are masters of gobbledyspook.)

Macbeth knows he is Thane of Glamis, but has no idea (or didn't have until now) of becoming Thane of Cawdor or King Hereafter. "Stay, you imperfect speakers, tell me more," he commands. But the witches, perhaps not liking the way he refers to their elocution, vanish into thin air, making it slightly thicker.

While Macbeth is meditating about what the witches have forecast for him, a couple of the King's henchmen, straight from a busy day of henching, ride up. They bring word that Duncan is liquidating the Thane of Cawdor and giving his title to Macbeth, it being an inexpensive gift.

"Look how our partner's rapt," remarks Banquo, noticing that Macbeth, stunned with all the good news, acts as if he has been struck on the noggin. But Macbeth is only lost in thought, and will find his way out presently. Thus far the witches have been batting 1.000, and Macbeth is beginning to take more than a casual interest in Duncan's health.[5]

Duncan is done in

Back at Macbeth's castle, Lady Macbeth receives a letter in which her husband tells about the witches and how prophetic their prophecies are proving. However, Lady Macbeth knows that her husband is a Weak Character. He would like to be king, but is embarrassed by any social unpleasantness, such as murdering a friend. Sometimes Lady Macbeth thinks there's something wrong with his circulatory system.

"It is too full o' the milk of human kindness," she mutters, remembering how easily his blood curdles. As for herself, she would ask nothing better than to be filled "from the crown to the toe, top-full of direst cruelty." She already has a good deal of the stuff in her, but thinks there is room for more.

Word comes that Duncan, on his way home from the battle and wanting to save the price of a hotel room, plans to spend the night with the Macbeths. Lady Macbeth rubs her hands with Glee, a Scottish detergent of those days, and prepares to entertain the royal guest. She seems to hear a raven

---

4. Until now it has been raining.
5. Henceforth when he says "How are you?" to the King it will be a bona fide question.

croaking, and that's a sure sign of death.[6]

By the time Macbeth arrives, Lady Macbeth has it all figured out. She tells her husband that they will wait until Duncan has gone to bed, ply his guards with drink, and then stab Duncan to death with the guards' daggers, thus not bloodying any of their own utensils.

Knowing that he shows everything on his face, including what he has eaten for breakfast, Lady Macbeth instructs her husband how to act. "Look like th' innocent flower," she says craftily, "but be the serpent under 't." Her last words are spoken with a menacing hiss.

Macbeth at first has misgivings, wondering whether this is quite the sort of thing for him to do as Duncan's host. Also he is scared, but not as scared as he is of Lady Macbeth.

"If it were done when 'tis done, then 'twere well it were done quickly," Macbeth rattles off to his wife, hoping to confuse her.

"Screw your courage to the sticking-place," Lady Macbeth tells him, handing him his tool box. Macbeth finally agrees to go along, but he doesn't sound any too enthusiastic.

"Is this a dagger which I see before me, the handle toward my hand?" Macbeth asks himself. (It is.) He hears a wolf howl, starts, and keeps going.

In a few moments an owl begins hooting, crickets cry,[7] and bells ring. Duncan, whom Macbeth has stabbed, is the only one who keeps still. Then Macbeth imagines he hears someone cry out, "Macbeth does murder sleep—the innocent sleep, sleep that knits up the raveled sleave[8] of care." This has become an FSQ[9] although carpers contend that it is nothing but a Mixed Metaphor.

Anyhow, he is too upset to put the bloody daggers by the guards, and Lady Macbeth takes over from her lily-livered husband.

"Screw your courage to the sticking-place," Lady Macbeth tells him, handing him his tool box.

"Infirm of purpose!" she addresses him tenderly, using a nickname she employs only when the two are alone together. "Give me the daggers." She carries them off, plants them by the guards, and is back in an instant, bloody but unbowed.

"I dare do all that may become a man," Macbeth says to her plaintively; "who dares do more is none." What he means is that it takes a woman to tackle the really dirty jobs. Just then a knocking is heard. At first Lady Macbeth thinks it's her husband's knees, but then she realizes the doorbell isn't working and somebody wants in.

"Retire we to our chamber," she whispers to Macbeth, who is staring at his hands as if he has never seen them before. Her idea is not to come out of retirement until they have removed all the telltale blood and climbed into their nighties. They exeunt.

The knocking continues, and a porter goes to the gate. He takes his time,[10] being busy speculating about Hell. (Shakespeare's porters are invariably Philosophers.) "Anon, anon," he calls to the persons outside, not

---

6. At least of the raven.
7. Usually they chirp, but not in a situation like this.
8. "Sleave," the scholars insist, is not the same as "sleeve," but no one is convinced.
9. Famous Shakespearean Quotation.
10. He is a porter, isn't he?

knowing their names.

The knockers are two of Duncan's henchmen—Macduff (in some texts Macduffel) and Lennox. They ask for Macbeth, and when he comes in, pretending to have been awakened by the uproar, they inquire about Duncan.

"Is he stirring?" asks Macduff.

"Not yet," Macbeth replies, having a hard time keeping a straight face. "'Twas a rough night," he adds, trying to explain his rather rumpled appearance.

Macduff goes into Duncan's room, and shortly thereafter dashes out looking as if he has seen a corpse.

"O horror, horror, horror!" he screams. As soon as he can think of another word, he cries, "Awake, awake!" Quickly he turns the place into bedlam. "Ring the bell! Come, look on death itself!" People begin to queue up. When Lady Macbeth enters and is told that Duncan is murdered, her reaction is studied.[11] "What, in our house?" she says, simulating horror at the choice of locale. "Help me hence, ho," she cries, confident that some courteous courtier will offer his arm. But too much else of interest is going on. Not until she swoons and lies stretched out on the floor does anyone pay her heed[12] and carry her out.

Naturally enough, the finger of suspicion points at the two guards, and Macbeth promptly kills them both before it swings around his way. Malcolm and Donalbain, Duncan's sons, don't like the look of things and light out for England and Ireland, respectively, before somebody puts the finger on them.

So Macbeth ascends the throne, and Lady Macbeth is terribly proud of her husband and the way he is going up in the world.

The ghostly guest

Macbeth should be happy as a king, but Banquo and his son Fleance disturb him. He remembers the witches' prophecy that Banquo is going to beget kings, and doesn't like the idea of having gone to all this trouble just to set up the throne for someone else's brats. Macbeth himself is the end of his line, and, although he doesn't know it yet, near the end of his rope. Besides, he suspects Banquo of suspecting him of foul play.[13]

So he invites Banquo to dine one evening at the castle. While Banquo and Fleance are out on a horseback ride, getting up an appetite,[14] Macbeth calls in a couple of professional and fully licensed murderers.[15] Any more murders on his own, he fears, will lose him his amateur standing. The murder-

---

11. Especially by young tragic actresses.
12. A small sum, or carrying charge.
13. By coincidence, "Foul play" is precisely what a contemporary reviewer, writing in the *London Tymes*, said of Macbeth.
14. Banquo has eaten at the castle before, and sitting at the same table with Lady Macbeth dries up his gastric juices.
15. Later joined by a third, thought by some scholars to be Macbeth in disguise, but more likely an apprentice murderer, getting experience.

ers, who are described as "without," though we never know what it is they lack, are quickly employed to practice their trade on Banquo and Fleance. They are despicable, heartless characters, and Macbeth is delighted to have made their acquaintance.

Banquo and Fleance are riding around and around in the park, still feeling none too hungry. The murderers wait until their victims have dismounted,[16] and then set upon Banquo and stab him fatally. Before he dies, however, he warns Fleance.

"Fly, good Fleance, fly, fly, fly!"

Obediently, Fleance takes off. Although he gains elevation only by leaps and bounds, he is soon out of sight. The murderers have accomplished only half the job, but for once it was the little one that got away.

That night, at the banquet, Macbeth is just sitting down when one of the murderers sticks his bloodstained face in, explaining that he cut himself while shaving. He reports to Macbeth that Banquo is done for, with twenty gashes in his head. But while they were counting the gashes, Fleance escaped, and they'll settle for fifty cents on the dollar.

Macbeth goes back to the table, intending to enjoy his mead and potatoes, but when he gets to his chair he sees the ghost of Banquo sitting in it. He is disconcerted, to say the least.

"See! Behold! Look! Lo!" he cries, but no one knows what's troubling him. They think he must be seeing things, which he is. Finally the ghost leaves, and Macbeth sits down, mopping his brow with a slab of roast beef. Lady Macbeth tries to calm everyone.

"My lord is often thus," she says soothingly, but creating an unfortunate picture of their home life. "The fit is momentary." Then she whispers into his ear, "Take care, my lord, thou'rt about to spill the beans."

Then she whispers into his ear, "Take care, my lord, thou'rt about to spill the beans."

Macbeth is just beginning to relax and regain his colour, when Banquo's ghost reenters.

"Avaunt, and quit my sight!" Macbeth screams. The ghost avaunts, but not before some of the guests.[17] Lady Macbeth suddenly yearns to be alone with her husband.

Alone, Macbeth and Lady Macbeth look at each other disconsolately. It will be hard to win back their reputation for gay dinner parties. The evening is ruined, and there is nothing left to do but go to bed and have a few nightmares.

The witches again

Macbeth is in deep now, and knows it. It was all caused by the rosy picture, now turned blood-red, painted by the witches. Maybe, thinks Macbeth, he can ask the weird sisters a few more questions and find out what's going to happen in the fifth act. Alone he strides the heath and, sure enough, comes upon the witches. These beauties are standing around a boiling caldron, fixing supper.

"Double, double toil and trouble," they moan as they stir the bubbling brew. Apparently they dislike cooking. As they stir, they toss in such ingredients as newts' eyes,

---

16. Shakespeare was part owner of the theatre, and well aware that the cleanup crew charged extra if a horse was brought onstage.

17. Macbeth is acting so insanely that he resembles Hamlet, and they fear they have stumbled into the wrong play.

goats' gall, poisoned entrails, bats' wool, lizards' legs, dragons' scales, and now and then the finger of a birth-strangled babe or a dash of baboon's blood for seasoning. They take care to follow the recipe[18] exactly, and, not surprisingly, seem in no rush to eat.

As Macbeth walks up, he hails them cheerily. "How now, you secret, black, and midnight hags!" He wants to ingratiate himself so they will answer his questions.

He seems to have said just the right thing, for they give him all sorts of interesting information. They advise him to look out for Macduff but otherwise not to worry, since (1) nobody born of woman shall harm him and (2) he won't be defeated until Birnam Wood comes to Dunsinane Hill. From this he gathers that he is an excellent insurance risk.

The only thing that disturbs Macbeth is a little pantomime staged by the witches shortly before they vanish. In it, Banquo's ghost points to a long row of kings, and grins sickeningly. Since the ghost may have been sampling the witches' bat and lizard stew, this is understandable. Macbeth correctly interprets the show to mean that Banquo has outfoxed and outbegot him. However, he still doesn't see how he can be defeated by the present generation. Though no student of obstetrics, he is afraid of no man not born of woman, and it is his considered opinion that Birnam Wood will stay put.

"Who can bid the tree unfix his earth-bound root?" he asks of no one in particular, and receives no answer.

Macbeth gets his

Although unable to get at Macduff, who is vacationing in England, Macbeth hires some murderers to slay Macduff's wife and son.[19] Fortunately most of this domestic slaughter takes place offstage.

When Macduff learns that his family has been wiped out, he is sore annoyed, which is an ugly combination. Teaming up with Duncan's son, Malcolm, he raises an army. This takes time—you know how long it takes to raise a family.

Meanwhile Lady Macbeth, who has been trying to remove Duncan's blood from her hands for weeks, keeps washing them without any luck.[20] When she isn't washing them, she is wringing them.

"Out, damned spot!" she shrieks, losing her temper and foolishly thinking an imprecation will succeed where cleaning fluid has failed. Self-possessed as she was in the first act, she is now a bundle of nerves, and none too securely tied together.

Night after night she walks in her sleep, muttering about blood and Banquo's ghost. Unfortunately the Court Doctor hasn't even a love seat, much less a couch, in his office. He is therefore "unable to minister to a mind diseased," and stands helplessly by.

"What's done cannot be undone," Lady

---

18. You can find this dish in Greta Ghoul's "Recipes for Retching" or in almost any diet cookbook.
19. The ready availability of murderers is a boon to Macbeth and to the plot.
20. See Glee above.

Macbeth mutters, struggling with a knot in her stomach. As she sleepwalks, she carries a candle in her hand, leaving a trail of tallow drippings.[21] Finally she dies, this being the only way she can give up the ghost.

Macduff, Malcolm, and their army are now at Birnam Wood, while Macbeth remains at his castle at Dunsinane. "Tomorrow, and tomorrow, and tomorrow," he says over and over and over to himself, rather liking the sound.

Alarum clocks commence to go off, signaling the beginning of the battle. Macbeth rushes to the field, still thinking he leads a charmed life. Only when the enemy soldiers camouflage themselves with trees from Birnam Wood and start branching out toward Dunsinane does Macbeth realize that the witches have played False with him. Then, when he gets into hand-to-hand, toe-to-toe conflict with Macduff, and Macduff casually mentions that he wasn't born of woman, or at least not in the usual way—he was "from his mother's womb untimely ripp'd" by some impatient obstetrician—Macbeth is ready to quit.

"Lay off, Macduff, I've had enuff"[22] is his unforgettable cry. But Macduff, warming to his task and sensing the final curtain, taunts his opponent.

"Yield thee, coward," he suggests, forgetting that Shakespearean heroes go down swinging.

Indeed, Macbeth has taken about all the guff from Macduff he can stand. "Lay on," he snarls, in a memorable change of prepositions.

The fighting is terrible, and it is fortunate for the audience that, like the slaughter of Lady Macduff and her son, it is offstage. They thrust, parry, and lunge as if their lives depend on it. At last Macbeth begins to tire. He is bored[23] by Macduff, who also cuts off his head. This he gives to Malcolm, who is now King of Scotland and likely to get all sorts of unusual presents.

As the curtain is rung down, Malcolm invites everyone to come and see him crowned at Scone. The invitation does not apply to members of the audience, who at this point are too exhausted, anyhow, for further festivities. ■

---

21. "Out, brief candle!" commands Macbeth, addressing an inanimate object (as do so many of Shakespeare's characters) in the full knowledge that it can't talk back.
22. Another version, no less authentic, is: "Lay ough, Macdough, I've had enough."
23. Through the heart.

In retelling the story of Macbeth, Armour utilizes a series of puns and word plays. Choose five puns that you think are especially clever. Choose another five that you would classify as "groaners."

Write Richard Armour expressing your opinion as to the value of his work being used in a classroom setting.

THE *Imagery* OF *Macbeth*

by Caroline Spurgeon

The imagery in *Macbeth* appears to me to be more imaginative, more subtle and complex than in other plays, and there are a greater number of ideas, interwoven the one with the other, recurring and repeating. There are at least three of these main ideas, and many subsidiary ones.

Clothing

One is the picture of Macbeth himself.

Few simple things—harmless in themselves—have such a curiously humiliating and degrading effect as the spectacle of a notably small man enveloped in a coat far too big for him. Comic actors know this well—Charlie Chaplin, for instance—and it is by means of this homely picture that Shakespeare shows us his imaginative view of the hero, and expresses the fact that the honours for which the murders were committed are, after all, of very little worth to him.

The idea constantly recurs that Macbeth's new honours sit ill upon him, like a loose and badly fitting garment, belonging to someone else. Macbeth himself first expresses it, quite early in the play, when, immediately following the first appearance of the witches and their prophecies, Ross arrives from the king, and greets him as thane of Cawdor, to which Macbeth quickly replies,

The thane of Cawdor lives: why do you
dress me
In borrow'd robes? (Act 1, sc. 3)

And a few minutes later, when he is rapt in ambitious thoughts suggested by the confirmation of two out of the three "prophetic greetings," Banquo, watching him, murmurs,

New honours come upon him,
Like our strange garments, cleave not to
their mould
But with the aid of use. (Act 1, sc. 3)

When Duncan is safely in the castle, Macbeth's better nature for a moment asserts itself, and, in debate with himself, he revolts from the contemplated deed for a threefold reason: because of its incalculable results, the treachery of such action from one who is both kinsman and host, and Duncan's own virtues and greatness as king.

When his wife joins him, his repugnance to the deed is as great, but it is significant that he gives three quite different reasons for not going ahead with it, reasons which he hopes may appeal to her, for he knows the others would not. So he urges that he has been lately honoured by the king, people think well of him, and therefore he should reap the reward of these things at once, and not upset everything by this murder which they have planned.

There is irony in the fact that to express the position he uses the same metaphor of clothes:

I have bought
Golden opinions from all sorts of people,
Which would be worn now in their newest gloss,
Not cast aside so soon. (Act 1, sc. 7)

To which Lady Macbeth, quite unmoved, retorts contemptuously:

Was the hope drunk
Wherein you dress'd yourself? (Act 1, sc. 7)

After the murder, when Ross says he is going to Scone for Macbeth's coronation, Macduff uses the same simile:

Well, may you see things well done there: adieu!
Lest our old robes sit easier than our new! (Act 2, sc. 4)

And, at the end, when the tyrant is at bay at Dunsinane, and the English troops are advancing, the Scottish lords still have this image in their minds. Caithness sees him as a man vainly trying to fasten a large garment on him with too small a belt:

He cannot buckle his distemper'd cause
Within the belt of rule; (Act 5, sc. 2)

while Angus, in a similar image, vividly sums up the essence of what they all have been thinking ever since Macbeth's accession to power:

now does he feel his title
Hang loose about him, like a giant's robe
Upon a dwarfish thief. (Act 5, sc. 2)

Undoubtedly Macbeth is built on great lines and in heroic proportions, with great possibilities—there could be no tragedy else. He is great, magnificently great, in courage, in passionate, indomitable ambition, in imagination and capacity to feel. But he could never be put beside, say Hamlet or Othello, in nobility of nature; and there *is* an aspect in which he is but a poor, vain, cruel, treacherous creature, snatching ruthlessly over the dead bodies of kinsman and friend at place and power he is utterly unfitted to possess. It is worth remembering that it is thus that Shakespeare, with his unshrinking clarity of vision, repeatedly sees him.

Light and Dark

Another constant idea in the play arises out of the symbolism that light stands for life, virtue, goodness; and darkness for evil and death. "Angels are bright," and witches are "secret, black and midnight hags," and the movement of the whole play might be summed up in the words, "good things of day begin to droop and drowse."

This is, of course, very obvious, but out of it develops the further thought which is assumed throughout, that the evil which is being done is so horrible that it would blast the sight to look on it; so that darkness, or partial blinding, is necessary to carry it out.

Like so much in the play it is ironic that it should be Duncan who first starts this simile, the idea of which turns into a leading motive in the tragedy. When he is conferring the new honour on his son, he is careful to say that others, kinsmen and thanes, will also be rewarded:

signs of nobleness, like stars, shall shine
On all deservers. (Act 1, sc. 4)

No sooner has the king spoken, than Macbeth realises that Malcolm, now a prince of the realm, is an added obstacle in his path, and suddenly, shrinking from the blazing horror of the murderous thought which follows, he cries to himself,

Stars, hide your fires;
Let not light see my black and deep desires. (Act 1, sc. 4)

From now on, the idea that only in darkness can such evil deeds be done is ever present with both Macbeth and his wife, as is seen in their two different and most characteristic invocations to darkness: her blood-curdling cry,

Come, thick night,
And pall thee in the dunnest smoke of
hell, (Act 1, sc. 5)

which takes added force when we hear later the poignant words, "She has light by her continually"; and his more gentle appeal in the language of falconry,

Come, seeling night,
Scarf up the tender eye of pitiful day.
(Act 3, sc. 2)

And when Banquo, sleepless, uneasy, with heart heavy as lead, crosses the courtyard on the fateful night, with Fleance holding the flaring torch before him, and, looking up to the dark sky, mutters,

There's husbandry in heaven,
Their candles are all out, (Act 2, sc. 1)

we know the scene is set for treachery and murder.

So it is fitting that on the day following, "dark night strangles the travelling lamp," (Act 2, sc. 7) and

darkness does the face of earth entomb,
When living light should kiss it. (Act 2, sc. 4)

The idea of deeds which are too terrible for human eyes to look on is also constant; Lady Macbeth scoffs it—"the sleeping and the dead," she argues, "are but as pictures":

'tis the eye of childhood
That fears a painted devil; (Act 2, sc. 2)

but Macduff, having seen the slain king, rushes out, and cries to Lennox,

Approach the chamber, and destroy your
sight
With a new Gorgon. (Act 2, sc. 3)

Macbeth boldly asserts he dare look on that "which might appal the devil," (Act 3, sc. 4) and the bitterness of defeat he realises on seeing one "too like the spirit of Banquo" in the procession of kings, is expressed in his agonised cry,

Thy crown does sear mine eye-balls;
(Act 4, sc. 1)

while in his bitter and beautiful words at the close, the dominant thoughts and images are the quenching of light and the empty reverberation of sound and fury, "signifying nothing." (Act 5, sc. 5)

Sickness

The third of the chief symbolic ideas in the play is one which is very constant with Shakespeare, and is to be found all through his work, that sin is a disease—Scotland is sick.

So Macbeth, while repudiating physic for himself, turns to the doctor and says if he could, by analysis, find Scotland's disease

And purge it to a sound and pristine
health,
I would applaud thee to the very echo,
That should applaud again...
What rhubarb, senna, or what purgative
drug,
Would scour these English hence?
(Act 5, sc. 3)

Malcolm speaks of his country as weeping, bleeding and wounded, and later urges Macduff to

make us medicines of our great revenge,
To cure this deadly grief; (Act 4, sc. 3)

while Caithness calls Malcolm himself the "medicine of the sickly weal," "the country's purge." (Act 5, sc. 2)

It is worth noting that all Macbeth's images of sickness are remedial or soothing in character: balm for a sore, sleep after fever, a purge, physic for pain, a "sweet oblivious antidote"; thus intensifying to the reader or audience his passionate and constant longing for well-being, rest, and, above all, peace of mind.

The Unnatural

Other subsidiary motives in the imagery, which work in and out through the play, insensibly but deeply affect the reader's imagination. One of these is the idea of the unnaturalness of Macbeth's crime, that it is a convulsion of nature. This is brought out repeatedly and emphasised by imagery, as are also the terrible results of going against nature.

Macbeth himself says that Duncan's wounds

look'd like a breach in nature
For ruin's wasteful entrance, (Act 2, sc. 3)

and Macduff speaks of his murder as the sacrilege of breaking open the Lord's anointed temple. (Act 2, sc. 3) The events which accompany and follow it are terrible because unnatural; an owl kills a falcon, horses eat each other, the earth was feverous and did shake, day becomes night; all this, says the old man, is unnatural,

Even like the deed that's done. (Act 2, sc. 4)

Macbeth's greatest trouble is the unnatural one that he has murdered sleep, (Act 2, sc. 2) and the whole feeling of dislocation is increased by such images as "let the frame of things disjoint," (Act 3, sc. 2) or by Macbeth's conjuration to the witches with the terrible list of the convulsions of nature which may result from their answering him. Indeed, if from one angle the movement of the play may be summed up in Macbeth's words,

Good things of day begin to droop and
drowse, (Act 3, sc. 2)

from another it is completely described by the doctor in his diagnosis of the doomed queen's malady as "a great perturbation in nature." (Act 5, sc. 1)

In addition to these images symbolising or expressing an idea, there are groups of others which might be called atmospheric in their effect, that is, they raise or increase certain feelings and emotions.

Blood

The feeling of fear, horror and pain is increased by the constant and recurring images of blood; these are very marked, and have been noticed by others, especially by Bradley, the most terrible being Macbeth's description of himself wading in a river of blood, while the most stirring to the imagination, perhaps in the whole of Shakespeare, is the picture of him gazing, rigid with horror, at his own blood-stained hand and watching it dye the whole green ocean red.

Animals

The images of animals also, nearly all predatory, unpleasant or fierce, add to this same feeling; such are a nest of scorpions, a venomous serpent and a snake, a "hell-kite" eating chickens, a devouring vulture, a swarm of insects, a tiger, rhinoceros and bear, the tiny wren fighting the owl for the life of her young, small birds with the fear of the net, lime, pitfall or gin, used with such bitter ironic effect by Lady Macduff and her boy just before they are murdered, the shrieking owl, and the bear tied to a stake fighting savagely to the end.

Enough has been said, I think, to indicate how complex and varied is the symbolism in the imagery of *Macbeth,* and to make it clear that an appreciable part of the emotions we feel throughout of pity, fear and horror, is due to the subtle but definite and repeated action of this imagery upon our minds, of which, in our preoccupation with the main theme, we remain often largely unconscious. ■

Spurgeon suggests that there are three main ideas developed through the imagery of the play. Create three collages, one for each of the ideas, which graphically illustrate the ideas. You may choose to combine magazine illustrations with your own art work. Be sure to include relevant words in your collages.

Can you think of any other ideas that are developed through the imagery in the play? Using Spurgeon's style as a model, write a short composition showing how imagery is used to develop a fourth idea in the play.

When was the Murder of Duncan First Plotted?

by A.C. Bradley

Did the Macbeths plot Duncan's murder before the meeting with the witches? In the following essay, two differing points of view are explored regarding this issue.

A good many readers probably think that, when Macbeth first met the Witches, he was perfectly innocent; but a much larger number would say that he had already harboured a vaguely guilty ambition, though he had not faced the idea of murder. And I think there can be no doubt that this is the obvious and natural interpretation of the scene. Only it is almost necessary to go rather further, and to suppose that his guilty ambition, whatever its precise form, was known to his wife and shared by her. Otherwise, surely, she would not, on reading his letter, so instantaneously assume that the King must be murdered in their castle; nor would Macbeth, as soon as he meets her, be aware (as he evidently is) that this thought is in her mind.

But there is a famous passage in *Macbeth* which, closely considered, seems to require us to go further still, and to suppose that, at some time before the action of the play begins, the husband and wife had explicitly discussed the idea of murdering Duncan at some favourable opportunity, and had agreed to execute this idea. Attention seems to have been first drawn to this passage by Koester in vol. I. of the *Johrbücher d. deutschen Shakespeare-Gesellschaft,* and on it is based the interpretation of the play in Werder's very able *Vorlesungen über Macbeth.*

The passage occurs in Act 1, sc. 7, where Lady Macbeth is urging her husband to the deed:

MACBETH Prithee, peace:
I dare do all that may become a man;
Who dares do more is none.
LADY MACBETH What beast was't, then,
That made you break this enterprise to me?
When you durst do it, then you were a man;
And, to be more than what you were, you would
Be so much more the man. Nor time nor place
Did then adhere, and yet you would make both:
They have made themselves, and that their fitness now
Does unmake you. I have given suck, and know
How tender 'tis to love the babe that milks me:
I would, while it was smiling in my face,

> Have pluck'd my nipple from his boneless gums,
> And dash'd the brains out, had I so sworn as you
> Have done to this.

Here Lady Macbeth asserts (1) that Macbeth proposed the murder to her: (2) that he did so at a time when there was no opportunity to attack Duncan, no 'adherence' of 'time' and 'place': (3) that he declared he would *make* an opportunity, and swore to carry out the murder.

Now it is possible that Macbeth's 'swearing' might have occurred in an interview off the stage between scenes 5 and 6 or scenes 6 and 7; and, if in that interview Lady Macbeth had with difficulty worked her husband up to a resolution, her irritation at his relapse, in sc. 7, would be very natural. But, as for Macbeth's first proposal of murder, it certainly does not occur in our play, nor could it possibly occur in any interview off the stage; for when Macbeth and his wife first meet, 'time' and 'place' *do* adhere; 'they have made themselves.' The conclusion would seem to be, either that the proposal of the murder and probably the oath, occurred in a scene at the very beginning of the play, which scene has been lost or cut out; or else that Macbeth proposed, and swore to execute, the murder at some time prior to the action of the play. The first of these hypotheses is most improbable, and we seem driven to adopt the second, unless we consent to burden Shakespeare with a careless mistake in a very critical passage.

"WHAT BEAST WAS'T, THEN, THAT MADE YOU BREAK THIS ENTERPRISE TO ME? WHEN YOU DURST DO IT, THEN YOU WERE A MAN; AND, TO BE MORE THAN WHAT YOU WERE, YOU WOULD. . ."

And, apart from unwillingness to do this, we can find a good deal to say in favour of a plan formed at a past time. It would explain Macbeth's start of fear at the prophecy of the kingdom. It would explain why Lady Macbeth, on receiving his letter, immediately resolves on action; and why, on their meeting, each knows that murder is in the mind of the other. And it is in harmony with her remarks on his probable shrinking from the act, to which *ex hypothesi,* she had already thought it necessary to make him pledge himself by an oath.

Yet I find it very difficult to believe in this interpretation. It is not merely that the interest of Macbeth's struggle with himself and with his wife would be seriously diminished if we felt he had been through all this before. I think this would be so; but there are two more important objections. In the first place the violent agitation described in the words,

> If good, why do I yield to that suggestion
> Whose horrid image doth unfix my hair
> And make my seated heart knock at my ribs,

would surely not be natural, even in Macbeth, if the idea of murder were already quite familiar to him through conversation with his wife, and if he had already done more than 'yield' to it. It is not as if the Witches had told him that Duncan was coming to his house. In that case the perception that the moment had come to execute a merely general design might well appal him. But all that he hears is that he will one day be King — a statement which, supposing this general design, would not point to any immediate action. And, in the second place, it is hard to believe that, if Shakespeare really had imagined the murder planned and sworn to before the action of the play, he would have written the first six scenes in such a manner that practically all readers imagine quite another state of affairs, *and continue to imagine it* even after they have read in scene 7 the passage which is troubling us. Is it likely, to put it otherwise, that his idea was one which nobody seems to have divined till late in the nineteenth century? And for what possible reason could he refrain from making this idea clear to his audience, as he might so easily have done in the third scene? It seems very much more likely that he himself imagined the matter as nearly all his readers do.

". . .Be so much more the man. Nor time nor place Did then adhere, and yet you would make both."

But, in that case, what are we to say of this passage? I will answer first by explaining the way in which I understood it before I was aware that it had caused so much difficulty. I suppose that an interview had taken place after scene 5, a scene which shows Macbeth shrinking, and in which his last words were 'we will speak further.' In this interview, I supposed, his wife had so wrought upon him that he had at last yielded and pledged himself by oath to do the murder. As for her statement that he had 'broken the enterprise' to her, I took it to refer to his letter to her—a letter written when time and place did not adhere, for he did not yet know that Duncan was coming to visit him. In the letter he does not, of course, openly 'break the enterprise' to her, and it is not likely that he would do such a thing in a letter; but if they had had ambitious conversations, in which each felt that some half-formed guilty idea was floating in the mind of the other she might naturally take the words of the letter as indicating much more than they said; and then in her passionate contempt at his hesitation, and her passionate eagerness to overcome it, she might easily accuse him, doubtless with exaggeration, and probably with conscious exaggeration, of having actually proposed the murder. And Macbeth, knowing that when he wrote the letter he really had been thinking of murder, and indifferent to anything except the question whether murder should be done, would easily let her statement pass unchallenged.

This interpretation still seems to me not unnatural. The alternative (unless we adopt the idea of an agreement prior to the action of the play) is to suppose that Lady Macbeth refers throughout the passage to some interview subsequent to her husband's return, and that, in making her do so, Shakespeare simply forgot her speeches on welcoming Macbeth home, and also forgot that at any such interview 'time' and 'place' did 'adhere.' It is easy to understand such forgetfulness in a spectator and even in a reader; but it is less easy to imagine it in a poet whose conception of the two characters throughout these scenes was evidently so burningly vivid. ■

What arguments does Bradley offer to support his claim that the Macbeths plotted the murder of Duncan before the encounter with the Weird Sisters? What arguments does he offer for the opposite point of view? Write a composition in which you state your views on the issue. Be sure to back up your opinions with details from the play or from Bradley's essay.

by Thomas De Quincey

On the KNOCKING *at the* GATE *in* MACBETH

In this classic essay from the 19th century, De Quincey explores his unbounded fascination with the knocking-at-the-gate scene in Macbeth.

From my boyish days I had always felt a great perplexity on one point in *Macbeth*. It was this: the knocking at the gate which succeeds to the murder of Duncan produced to my feelings an effect for which I never could account. The effect was that it reflected back upon the murderer a peculiar awfulness and a depth of solemnity; yet, however obstinately I endeavored with my understanding to comprehend this, for many years I never could see why it should produce such an effect.

My understanding could furnish no reason why the knocking at the gate in *Macbeth* should produce any effect, direct or reflected. In fact, my understanding said positively that it could *not* produce any effect. But I knew better; I felt that it did; and I waited and clung to the problem until further knowledge should enable me to solve it.....

My solution is this—murder, in ordinary cases, where the sympathy is wholly directed to the case of the murdered person, is an incident of coarse and vulgar horror; and for this reason—that it flings the interest exclusively upon the natural but ignoble instinct by which we cleave to life: an instinct which, as being indispensable to the primal law of self-preservation, is the same in kind (though different in degree) amongst all living creatures. This instinct exhibits human nature in its most abject and humiliating attitude. Such an attitude would little suit the purposes of the poet.

What then must he do? He must throw the interest on the murderer. Our sympathy must be with *him* (of course I mean a sympathy of comprehension, a sympathy by which we enter into his feelings, and are made to understand them—not a sympathy of pity or approbation). In the murdered person all strife of thought, all flux and reflux of passion and of purpose, are crushed by one overwhelming panic. But in the murderer, such a murderer as a poet will condescend to, there must be raging some great storm of passion—jealousy, ambition, vengeance, hatred—which will create a hell within him; and into this hell we are to look.

In *Macbeth,* Shakespeare has introduced two murderers; and, as usual in his hands, they are remarkably discriminated: but—though in Macbeth the strife of mind is greater than in his wife, the tiger spirit not so awake, and his feelings caught chiefly by contagion from her—yet, as both were finally involved in the guilt of murder, the murderous mind of necessity is finally to be presumed in both. We were to be made to feel that the human nature—i.e., the divine nature of love and mercy, spread through the hearts of all creatures, and seldom utterly withdrawn from man—was gone, vanished, extinct, and that the fiendish nature had taken its place.

If the reader has ever been present in a vast metropolis on the day when some great national idol was carried in funeral pomp to his grave, and, chancing to walk near the course through which it passed, has felt powerfully, in the silence and desertion of the streets and in the stagnation of ordinary business, the deep interest which at that moment was possessing the heart of man—if all at once he should hear the death-like stillness broken up by the sound of wheels rattling away from the scene, and making known that the transitory vision was dissolved, he will be aware that at no moment was his sense of the complete suspension and pause in ordinary human concerns so full and affecting as at that moment when the suspension ceases, and the goings-on of human life are suddenly resumed. All action in any direction is best expounded, measured, and made apprehensible, by reaction.

Now apply this to the case in Macbeth. Here, as I have said, the retiring of the human heart and the entrance of the fiendish heart was to be expressed and made sensible. Another world has stepped in; and the murderers are taken out of the region of human things, human purposes, human desires. They are transfigured: Lady Macbeth is "unsexed"; Macbeth has forgot that he was born of woman; both are conformed to the image of devils; and the world of devils is suddenly revealed. But how shall this to be conveyed and made palpable? In order that a new world may step in, this world must for a time disappear. The murderers, and the murder, must be insulated—cut off by an immeasurable gulf from the ordinary tide and succession of human affairs—locked up and sequestered in some deep recess; we must be made sensible that the world of ordinary life is suddenly arrested—laid asleep—tranced—racked into a dread armistice; time must be annihilated; relation to things without abolished; and all must pass self-withdrawn into a deep syncope and suspension of earthly passion. Hence it is that, when the deed is done, when the work of darkness is perfect, then the world of darkness passes away like a pageantry in the clouds: the knocking at the gate is heard, and it makes known audibly that the reaction has commenced; the human has made its reflux upon the fiendish: the pulses of life are beginning to beat again; and the re-establishment of the goings-on of the world in which we live first makes us profoundly sensible of the awful parenthesis that had suspended them.

O mighty poet! Thy works are not as those of other men, simply and merely great works of art, but are also like the phenomena of nature, like the sun and the sea, the stars and the flowers, like frost and snow, rain and dew, hail-storm and thunder, which are to be studied with entire submission of our own faculties, and in the perfect faith that in them there can be no too much or too little, nothing useless or inert, but that, the farther we press in our discoveries, the more we shall see proofs of design and self-supporting arrangement where the careless eye had seen nothing but accident! ■

Summarize in your own words why the knocking at the gate has such a powerful effect on De Quincey.

The last paragraph of this literary reflection is quite poetic, to say the least. Turn this piece of prose into a "found poem" by arranging the words so that the paragraph looks like poetry.

by James Thurber

The Macbeth Murder Mystery

Who really killed Duncan and who exactly is the Third Murderer? Is there more to the story of Macbeth than meets the eye?

"It was a stupid mistake to make," said the American woman I had met at my hotel in the English lake country, "but it was on the counter with the other Penguin books—the little sixpenny ones, you know, with the paper covers—and I supposed of course it was a detective story. All the others were detective stories. I'd read all the others, so I bought this one without really looking at it carefully. You can imagine how mad I was when I found it was Shakespeare." I murmured something sympathetically. "I don't see why the Penguin-books people had to get out Shakespeare plays in the same size and everything as the detective stories," went on my companion. "I think they have different-colored jackets," I said. "Well, I didn't notice that," she said. "Anyway, I got real comfy in bed that night and all ready to read a good mystery story and here I had 'The Tragedy of Macbeth'—a book for high school students. Like 'Ivanhoe.'" "Or 'Lorna Doone,'" I said. "Exactly," said the American lady. "And I was just crazy for a good Agatha Christie, or something. Hercule Poirot is my favorite detective." "Is he the rabbity one?" I asked. "Oh, no," said my crime-fiction expert. "He's the Belgian one. You're thinking of Mr. Pinkerton, the one that helps Inspector Bull. He's good, too."

Over her second cup of tea my companion began to tell the plot of a detective story that had fooled her completely—it seems it was the old family doctor all the time. But I cut in on her. "Tell me," I said. "Did you read 'Macbeth'?" "I had to read it," she said. "There wasn't a scrap of anything else to read in the whole room." "Did you like it?" I asked. "No, I did not," she said, decisively. "In the first place, I don't think for a moment that Macbeth did it." I looked at her blankly. "Did what?" I asked. "I don't think for a moment that he killed the King," she said. "I don't think the Macbeth woman was mixed up in it, either. You suspect them the most, of course, but those are the ones that are never guilty—or shouldn't be, anyway." "I'm afraid," I began, "that I—" "But don't you see?" said the American lady. "It would spoil everything if you could figure out right away who did it. Shakespeare was too smart for that. I've read that people never *have* figured out 'Hamlet,' so it isn't likely Shakespeare would have made 'Macbeth' as simple as it seems." I thought this over while I filled my pipe. "Who do you suspect?" I asked, suddenly. "Macduff," she said, promptly. "Good God!" I whispered, softly.

"Oh Macduff did it, all right," said the murder specialist. "Hercule Poirot would have got him easily." "How did you figure it out?" I demanded. "Well," she said, "I didn't right away. At first I suspected Banquo. And then, of course, he was the second person killed. That was good right in there, that part. The person you suspect of the first murder should always be the second victim." "Is that so?" I murmured. "Oh, yes," said my informant. "They have to keep surprising you. Well, after the second murder I didn't know *who* the killer was for a while." "How about Malcolm and Donalbain, the King's sons?" I asked. "As I remember it, they fled right after the first murder. That looks suspicious." "Too suspicious," said the American lady. "Much too suspicious. When they flee, they're never guilty. You can count on that." "I believe," I said, "I'll have a brandy," and I summoned the waiter. My companion leaned toward me, her eyes bright, her teacup quivering. "Do you know who discovered Duncan's body?" she demanded. I said I was sorry, but I had forgotten. "Macduff discovers it," she said, slipping into the historical present. "Then he comes running downstairs and shouts, 'Confusion has broke open the Lord's anointed temple' and 'Sacrilegious murder has made his masterpiece' and on and on like that." The good lady tapped me on the knee. "All that stuff was rehearsed," she said. "You wouldn't say a lot of stuff like that, offhand, would you—if you had found a body?" She fixed me with a glittering eye. "I—" I began. "You're right!" she said. "You wouldn't! Unless you had practiced it in advance. 'My God, there's a body in here!' is what an innocent man would say." She sat back with a confident glare.

I thought for a while. "But what do you make of the Third Murderer?" I asked. "You know, the Third Murderer has puzzled 'Macbeth' scholars for 300 years." "That's because they never thought of Macduff," said the American lady. "It was Macduff, I'm certain. You couldn't have one of the victims murdered by two ordinary thugs—the murderer always has to be somebody important." "But what about the banquet scene?" I asked, after a moment. "How do you account for Macbeth's guilty actions there, when Banquo's ghost came in and sat in his chair?" The lady leaned forward and tapped me on the knee again. "There wasn't any ghost," she said. "A big, strong man like that doesn't go around seeing ghosts—especially in a brightly lighted banquet hall with dozens of people around. Macbeth was *shielding somebody!*" "Who was he shielding?" I asked. "Mrs. Macbeth, of course," she said. "He thought she did it and he was going to take the rap himself. The husband always does that when the wife is suspected." "But what," I demanded, "about the sleepwalking scene, then?" "The same thing, only the other way around," said my companion. "That time *she* was shielding *him*. She wasn't asleep at all. Do you remember where it says, 'Enter Lady Macbeth with a taper'?" "Yes," I said. "Well, people who walk in their sleep *never carry lights!*" said my fellow-traveler. "They have a second sight. Did you ever hear of a

"A big, strong man like that doesn't go around seeing ghosts—especially in a brightly lighted banquet hall with dozens of people around."

sleepwalker carrying a light?" "No," I said, "I never did." "Well, then, she wasn't asleep. She was acting guilty to shield Macbeth." "I think," I said, "I'll have another brandy," and I called the waiter. When he brought it, I drank it rapidly and rose to go. "I believe," I said, "that you have got hold of something. Would you lend me that 'Macbeth'? I'd like to look it over tonight. I don't feel, somehow, as if I'd ever really read it." "I'll get it for you," she said. "But you'll find that I am right."

I read the play over carefully that night, and the next morning, after breakfast, I sought out the American woman. She was on the putting green, and I came up behind her silently and took her arm. She gave an exclamation. "Could I see you alone?" I asked, in a low voice. She nodded cautiously and followed me to a secluded spot. "You've found out something?" she breathed. "I've found out," I said, triumphantly, "the name of the murderer!" "You mean it wasn't Macduff?" she said. "Macduff is as innocent of those murders," I said, "as Macbeth and the Macbeth woman." I opened the copy of the play, which I had with me, and turned to Act II, Scene 2. "Here," I said, "you will see where Lady Macbeth says, 'I laid their daggers ready. He could not miss 'em. Had he not resembled my father as he slept, I had done it.' Do you see?" "No," said the American woman, bluntly, "I don't." "But it's simple!" I exclaimed. "I wonder I didn't see it years ago. The reason Duncan resembled Lady Macbeth's father as he slept is that *it actually was her father!*" "Good God!" breathed my companion, softly. "Lady Macbeth's father killed the King," I said, "and, hearing someone coming, thrust the body under the bed and crawled into the bed himself." "But," said the lady, "you can't have a murderer who only appears in the story once. You can't have that." "I know that," I said, and I turned to Act II, Scene 4. "It says here, 'Enter Ross with an old Man.' Now, that old man is never identified and it is my contention he was old Mr. Macbeth, whose ambition it was to make his daughter Queen. There you have your motive." "But even then," cried the American lady, "he's still a minor character!" "Not," I said, gleefully, "when you realize that he was also *one of the weird sisters in disguise!*" "You mean one of the three witches?" "Precisely," I said. "Listen to this speech of the old man's. 'On Tuesday last, a falcon towering in her pride of place, was by a mousing owl hawk'd at and killed.' Who does that sound like?" "It sounds like the way the three witches talk," said my companion, reluctantly. "Precisely!" I said again. "Well," said the American woman, "maybe you're right, but—" "I'm sure I am," I said. "And do you know what I'm going to do now?" "No," she said. "What?" "Buy a copy of 'Hamlet,'" I said, "and solve *that!*" My companion's eye brightened. "Then," she said, "you don't think Hamlet did it?" "I am," I said, "absolutely positive he didn't." "But who," she demanded, "do you suspect?" I looked at her cryptically. "Everybody," I said, and disappeared into a small grove of trees as silently as I had come. ■

How plausible are the two alternative scenarios offered in this story? Which do you think is more convincing? What other evidence would you offer to support your view?

The story suggests that at least two other people are prime suspects in the murder of Duncan. Continue Thurber's story and build a case for a different suspect.

by Harold C. Goddard

MACBETH *as the* Third MURDERER

Here are some compelling arguments that may even convince you that Macbeth was the Third Murderer!

I do not intend to defend the view that Macbeth was the Third Murderer—or that he was not. I wish rather to call attention to a remarkable fact concerning the response of readers to this question. Over the years I have called the attention of hundreds to it, most of whom had never heard of it before. It seems to exercise a peculiar fascination and to set even ordinarily casual readers to scanning the text with the minutest attention. And to what conclusion do they come? With a small group no one can predict. But with numbers sufficient to permit the law of averages to apply, the results have an almost scientific consistency. After allowing for a small minority that remains in doubt, about half are convinced that Macbeth was the Third Murderer and the other half are either unconvinced or frankly think the hypothesis farfetched or absurd.

And who killed Banquo? Is it the cat's paw that pulls the chestnuts from the fire, or he who holds the cat and guides the paw?

But if the idea that Macbeth was the Third Murderer never entered Shakespeare's head, by what autonomous action of language does the text take on a meaning to the contrary that convinces nearly half of the play's readers? And not only convinces them, but, on the whole, convinces them for the same reasons. That without any basis hundreds should be deluded in the same way is unthinkable. But why, then, it will be asked, did not Shakespeare make his intention plain?—a question that reveals a peculiar insensitivity to poetry. What the poet wanted, evidently, was not to make a bald identification of the two men but to produce precisely the effect which as a matter of fact the text does produce on sensitive but unanalytic readers, the feeling, namely, that there is something strange and spectral about the Third Murderer as, unexpected and unannounced, he appears at this remote spot where

The west yet glimmers with some
streaks of day.

Utter darkness is imminent. Now is the time when the last streaks of day in Macbeth's nature are about to fade out forever—and here is the place. Whether he is present or absent in the flesh, it is here and now that he steps through the door above which is written "Abandon all hope, ye who enter."

The author must convince us that virtually, if not literally, it is Macbeth who commits the murder. By letting us unconsciously see things simultaneously from two angles, he creates, as sight with two eyes does in the physical world, the true illusion of another dimension, in this case an illusion that annihilates space.

Macbeth's body—who knows?—may have been shut up in his chamber at the palace. But where was the man himself—his ambition, his fear, his straining inner vision, his will? They were so utterly with the hired instruments of that will that we can almost imagine them capable of incarnating themselves in a spectral body and projecting themselves as an apparition to the other two. And who killed Banquo? Is it the cat's paw that pulls the chestnuts from the fire, or he who holds the cat and guides the paw? So here. And we must be made to feel it—whatever we think. It is the poet's duty to bring the spirit of Macbeth to life on the scene. He does.

How he does it is worth pausing a moment to notice—in so far as anything so subtle can be analyzed—for it reveals in miniature the secret of his power over our imaginations throughout the play.

The Third Murderer speaks six times. All but one of his speeches—and that one is but two lines and a half—are brief, one of one word only, and one of two. And every one of these speeches either has something in it to remind us of Macbeth, or might have been spoken to him, or both.

1. When the First Murderer, disturbed, asks who bade him join them, his Delphic answer is: Macbeth.

2. He is the first to hear the approaching Banquo: Hark! I hear horses.

The horse, *that on which we ride,* as we have noted elsewhere, is one of the oldest symbols of the unconscious, and that this very symbol is in a highly activated state in Macbeth's mind Shakespeare has been careful to note from his "pity, like a naked new-born babe, striding the blast," and "heaven's cherubin, hors'd upon the sightless couriers of the air" onward. Later, when messengers bring word of Macduff's flight to England, Macbeth's imaginative ear evidently catches the galloping of their horses before it rises above the threshold of consciousness and he translates it into supernatural terms:

MACBETH Saw you the weïrd sisters?
LENNOX No, my lord.
MACBETH Came they not by you?
LENNOX No, indeed, my lord.
MACBETH Infected be the air whereon they ride,
And damn'd all those that trust them! I did hear
the galloping of horse: who was't came by?
LENNOX 'Tis two or three, my lord, that bring you word Macduff is fled to England.

The Weïrd Sisters could not have been far off, either, when Banquo was murdered. It is interesting, to say the least, that it is the Third Murderer who first hears the horses. Whoever he is, he is like Macbeth in being sensitive to sound. He and Macbeth, it might be said, hear ear to ear.

3. The Third Murderer's next speech is his longest. To the First Murderer's "His horses go about," he replies:

Almost a mile; but he does usually—
So all men do—from hence to the palace gate
Make it their walk.

Dashes, in place of the more usual commas, help bring out what is plainly a slip of the tongue on the Third Murderer's part. He has begun to reveal what in the circumstances is a suspicious familiarity with Banquo's habits, when, realizing his mistake, he hurriedly tries to cover it with his plainly parenthetical "so all men do" and his consequently necessary substitution of "their" for "his." But Macbeth does much the same thing just before the murder of Duncan is discovered:

LENNOX Goes the king hence today?
MACBETH He does—he did appoint so.

"He does usually—so all men do." "He does—he did appoint so." Such an echo sounds almost as if it came from the same voice. Only someone like Macbeth in combined impulsiveness and quick repentance of impulsiveness could have spoken the Third Murderer's words.

4. The fourth speech confirms the third:

'Tis he.

He is the first to recognize Banquo.

5. "Who did strike out the light?" Who *did?* Is it possible that one of the cutthroats is quite willing to kill a man but balks at the murder of a child? We do not know. But it does not need the King's "Give me some light!" in *Hamlet* or Othello's

Put out the light, and then put out the
light,

to make us aware of a second meaning in this simple question. It was the question that Macbeth must never have ceased to ask himself as he went on down into utter darkness.

6. "There's but one down; the son is fled." The Third Murderer is more perturbed than the others at the escape of Fleance. When at the beginning of the next scene Macbeth learns from the First Murderer of the death of the father and the flight of the son, he cries:

Then comes my fit again. I had else been
perfect,
Whole as the marble, founded as the
rock,
As broad and general as the casing air;
But now I am cabin'd, cribb'd, confin'd,
bound in
To saucy doubts and fears.

It is mainly on this speech that those who hold absurd the idea that Macbeth was the Third Murderer rest their case, proof, they say, that the news of Fleance's escape came to him as a surprise. But others think the lines have the same marks of insincerity combined with unconscious truth as those in which Macbeth pretended to be surprised and horrified at the death of Duncan.

All this about the Third Murderer will be particularly abhorrent to "realists," who would bring everything to the bar of the senses, and logicians, whose fundamental axiom is that a thing cannot both be and not be at the same time. One wonders if they never had a dream in which one of the actors both was and was not a character from so-called "real" life. Anything that can happen in a dream can happen in poetry. Indeed this scene in which Banquo dies seems one of the most remarkable confirmations in Shakespeare that dreams and the drama come out of a common root. When an audience gathers in a theatre, they come, if the play is worthy of the theater's great tradition, not to behold a transcript of the same old daylight life, but to dream together. In his bed a man dreaming is cut off from all social life. In the theatre he is dreaming one dream with his fellows. ■

Which of Goddard's arguments are the most compelling in building a case for Macbeth as the Third Murderer? Which are the least?

Write Goddard a letter in which you outline how you feel about his argument for Macbeth as the Third Murderer.

James I. (1603–25)

by Rudyard Kipling

Some people believe that Shakespeare wrote Macbeth to please James I. Kipling here provides a portrait of what this Scottish king of England was really like.

The child of Mary Queen of Scots,
A shifty mother's shiftless son,
Bred up among intrigues and plots,
Learned in all things, wise in none.
Ungainly, babbling, wasteful, weak,
Shrewd, clever, cowardly, pedantic,
The sight of steel would blanch his cheek.
The smell of baccy drive him frantic.
He was the author of his line—
He wrote that witches should be burnt;
He wrote that monarchs were divine,
And left a son who—proved they weren't!

Kipling does not offer us a very attractive portrait of James I. Conduct some research to expand upon the information provided in each line of the poem. What were his views on witchcraft? Did he deserve the criticism levelled at him by Kipling?

by William Davenant

A Scene Left Out of Shakespeare's Macbeth

Sir William Davenant (1606 – 1668) bragged frequently that he was Shakespeare's illegitimate son. Although there is little if anything to back this claim, Davenant lived a full life in the theatre and even adapted a number of Shakespeare's plays including Macbeth.

Enter Macduff and Lady Macduff.

LADY MACDUFF: Are you resolved then to be gone?
MACDUFF: I am.
I know my answer cannot but inflame
The tyrant's fury to pronounce my death.
My life will soon be blasted by his breath.
LADY MACDUFF: But why so far as England must you fly?
MACDUFF: The farthest part of Scotland is too nigh.
LADY MACDUFF: Can you leave me, your daughter, and your son
To perish by that tempest which you shun?
When birds of stronger wing are fled away
The ravenous kite does on the weaker, prey.
MACDUFF: He will not injure you. He cannot be
Possessed with such unmanly cruelty.
You will safety to your weakness owe
As grass escapes the scythe by being low.
Together we shall be too slow to fly
Single we may out-ride the enemy
I'll from the English King such succours crave
As shall revenge the dead, and living save.
My greatest misery is to remove
With all the wings of haste from what I love
LADY MACDUFF: If to be gone seems misery to you
Good sir let us be miserable too
MACDUFF: Your sex, which here is your security
Will by the toils of flight your danger be.

Enter Messenger.

What fatal news does bring thee out of breath?
Messenger: Sir Banquo is killed.
Macduff: Then I am warned of death.
Farewell, our safety us a while must sever.
Lady Macduff: Fly, fly or we may bid farewell for ever.
Macduff: Flying from death I am to life unkind,
For leaving you I leave my life behind.

Exit.

Lady Macduff: Oh my dear Lord, I find now thou art gone,
I am more valiant when unsafe alone.
My heart feels manhood. It does death despise,
Yet I am still a woman in my eyes
And of my tears thy absence is the cause
So falls the dew when the bright sun withdraws.

When Davenant adapted Shakespeare's *Macbeth,* he changed most of Shakespeare's lines, he cut scenes and added scenes that he felt were missing from the original. Can you think of any other scenes that are "missing" from the play? Using Shakespeare or Davenant as a model, write a scene that you think has been left out of the play.

by Robert Frost

"Out, Out—"

"Don't let him cut my hand off" pleads the young boy. Like Macbeth, "he saw all spoiled" before he entered "the dark of ether."

The buzz-saw snarled and rattled in the yard
And made dust and dropped stove-length sticks of wood,
Sweet-scented stuff, when the breeze drew across it.
And from there those that lifted eyes could count
Five mountain ranges one behind the other
Under the sunset far into Vermont.
And the saw snarled and rattled, snarled and rattled,
As it ran light, or had to bear a load.
And nothing happened: day was all but done.
Call it a day, I wish they might have said
To please the boy by giving him the half hour
That a boy counts so much when saved from work.
His sister stood beside them in her apron
To tell them 'Supper.' At the word, the saw,
As if to prove saws knew what supper meant,
Leaped out at the boy's hand, or seemed to leap—
He must have given the hand. However it was,
Neither refused the meeting. But the hand!
The boy's first outcry was a rueful laugh,
As he swung toward them holding up the hand
Half in appeal, but half as if to keep
The life from spilling. Then the boy saw all—
Since he was old enough to know, big boy
Doing a man's work, though a child at heart—

He saw all spoiled. 'Don't let him cut my hand off—
The doctor, when he comes. Don't let him, sister!'
So. But the hand was gone already.
The doctor put him in the dark of ether.
He lay and puffed his lips out with his breath.
And then—the watcher at his pulse took fright.
No one believed. They listened at his heart.
Little—less—nothing!—and that ended it.
No more to build on there. And they, since they
Were not the one dead, turned to their affairs.

In pairs, discuss the appropriateness of the title of this poem. Consider all the reasons you can to justify the use of the allusion to Macbeth's speech as the title of the poem.

If "Out, Out ..." were not the title of this poem, what other line from *Macbeth* would you suggest in its place?

At the Fire and Cauldron Health-Food Restaurant

by Martin Robbins

The Weird Sisters aren't the only ones who know how to "serve a strange buffet."

Here we serve a strange buffet:
tender snake and shark fillet;
eye of newt, and toe of frog,
wool of bat, and tongue of dog.
Bubble, bubble, it's worth our trouble,
organic cooking costs you double.

Daily specials packed with health,
stuff we've gathered up with stealth:
adder's fork and blindworm's sting,
lizard's leg and howlet's wing.
Fire burn and cauldron bubble,
our food charms your stomach trouble.

Buzzard's nest soup or witches' brew,
moon-grown mushrooms grace our stew:
fill your plate with healthful weeds,
burdock root and fennel seeds.
In thunder, lightning or in rain,
we'll fix old potions for your pain.

Here we mix our recipes
stocked from nature's pharmacies:
order food medicinal
at the Weird Sisters' table.
We don't give you paper fortunes,
here you'll see your future's portents.

Change your past, with what you eat:
give up beef, it's not too late.
Munch on grains, we cook 'em whole,
cow gas spreads the ozone hole.
Forest stubble, fear and trouble,
heaven burns, your planet bubbles.

Write your own parody of the "Double, double, toil and trouble" chant. Choose a setting where one would expect to find strange ingredients being mixed together.

Three Tragic THEMES

by Edith Sitwell

"In this vast world torn from the universe of night ..." So begins renowned English poet Edith Sitwell's excursion into the themes of Macbeth.

In this vast world torn from the universe of night, there are three tragic themes. The first theme is that of the actual guilt, and the separation in damnation of the two characters—the man who, in spite of his guilt, walks the road of the spirit, and who loves the light that has forsaken him—and the woman who, after her invocation to the "Spirits who tend on mortall thoughts," walks in the material world, and who does not know that light exists, until she is nearing her end and must seek the comfort of one small taper to illumine all the murkiness of Hell.

The second tragic theme of the play is the man's love for the woman whose damnation is of the earth, who is unable, until death is near, to conceive of the damnation of the spirit, and who in her blindness therefore strays away from him, leaving him for ever in his lonely hell.

The third tragic theme is the woman's despairing love for the man whose vision she cannot see, and whom she has helped to drive into damnation.

The very voices of these two damned souls have therefore a different sound. His voice is like that of some gigantic being in torment—of a lion with a human soul. In her speech invoking darkness, the actual sound is so murky and thick that the lines seem impervious to light, and, at times, rusty, as though they had lain in the blood that had been spilt, or in some hell-born dew. There is no escape from what we have done. The past will return to confront us. ■

Edith Sitwell is best known for her poetry. This excerpt from her "Notebook on William Shakespeare" provides testimony for her poetic accomplishments. Write a poem or series of poems in which you explore any or all of the three themes identified by Sitwell. You may, if you wish, use short phrases from this selection in your verse.

by Lisa Low

Ridding Ourselves of Macbeth

Despite the fact that Macbeth is a ruthless butcher and bloody fiend, we find ourselves drawn to him. How does Shakespeare succeed in accomplishing this reaction?

But where there is danger,
There grows also what saves.
—*Hölderlin*

Unlike most tragic heroes, Macbeth is much less sinned against than sinning, which makes him a strange candidate for our affections. He does not fall prey to infirmity like Lear, nor is he ignorant of what he does like Oedipus. He is not like Romeo, well-intentioned but too hasty; nor is he like Hamlet, Romeo's inverse, too cool. Too hot to stop, too cool to feel. Macbeth is no Romeo and no Hamlet. He is a fiend and a butcher. Standing before him, we cannot but be paralyzed with fear.

Macbeth is no Romeo and no Hamlet. He is a fiend and a butcher. Standing before him, we cannot but be paralyzed with fear.

And yet, almost against our wills, we are drawn to Macbeth. We should not be, but we are. We are with him in his darkest hours and though we cannot especially hope for his success, we share with him the uncomfortable feeling that what must be done must be done and that what has been done cannot be undone. Banquo, who we come to feel is a threat to ourselves, however good, must be eliminated. So must Fleance, Macduff's wife and children, or anyone else who stands in the highway of our intense progress. Thinking that "to be thus is nothing, but to be safely thus," and wishing with "barefaced power" to sweep him from our sights, we straddle the play repelled by, but irresistibly drawn to Macbeth.

We listen to Macbeth as we listen to the beatings of our hearts. Engaged in the play, we think our hands are up to the wrists in blood and we startle at the knockings at our doors. Watching Macbeth, we suspect the height and depth of our own evil, testing ourselves up to the waist in the waters of some bloody lake. Allowed to do that which we must not do, guaranteed that we shall suffer for it, we watch Macbeth by laying our ears up against the door where our own silent nightmares are proceeding. There we see ourselves projected, gone somehow suddenly wrong, participating in the unforgivable, pursued by the unforgiving, which is most of all, ourselves.

Why should this be? Why are we so drawn to Macbeth by whom we must be at last repelled? Two reasons suggest themselves. First, we identify with Macbeth because identification is the condition of the theatre, especially in a nearly expressionistic play like *Macbeth* where the stage is the meeting ground between the hero's psyche and ours. Second, we pity Macbeth because, like us, he moves within breathing distance of innocence.

As moral obscurity is the world in which Macbeth stands at the beginning of his play, so it is the world in which we are seated watching the play, for the stage is both an extension of Macbeth's mind and the field of our imaginations. There in the domed, dimly lit theatre we watch like swaddled infants, this two hours' traffic, this our own strutting and fretting upon a bloody stage. Before us the Macbeths move like shadowy players, brief candles, little vaporous forms sliding behind a scrim. As if standing in Plato's cave, we see, but at one remove, we listen, but only to echoes, until we find ourselves fumbling along the corridors of our own dark psyches. There, supping on evil, dipped to the waist in blood, we watch the Macbeths go out at last in a clatter of sound, pursued by furies. The play over and the brief candles out, night flees, vapors vanish, and light is restored.

We identify with Macbeth because the theatre makes us suffer the illusion that we are Macbeth. We pity him because, like us, he stands next to innocence in a world in which evil is a prerequisite for being human. Macbeth is not motivelessly malicious. He savors no sadistic pleasure in cruelty. Rather, set within reach of glory, he reaches and falls, and falling he is sick with remorse.

To have a clear conscience is to stand in the sun. To have a clouded conscience, one hovering between good and evil, between desire and restraint, is to stand where most of us stand, in that strange and obscure purgatory where the wind is pocketed with hot and cool trends, where the air is not nimble and sweet but fair and foul. This is the world of choice where thought and act and hand and eye are knit, but in a system of checks and balances.

Set within reach of triumph, who is not tempted to reach? And who, plucking one, will not compulsively and helplessly pluck every apple from the apple tree? For the line dividing self-preservation from ambition is often thin and we walk as if on a narrow cord above an abyss. We have constantly to choose, almost against our wills, for good, for it is easier to fall than to fly. We identify with Macbeth because we live in a dangerous world where a slip is likely to be a fall; but in the end, we must rip ourselves from him violently, as of a curse, as of an intolerable knowledge of ourselves. Through him we pay our chief debts to the unthinkable and are washed, when we wake, up onto the white shores of our own innocence. ■

Lisa Low claims that we are irresistibly drawn to Macbeth. Do you agree? Write a letter to Low expressing how you feel about the ideas she describes in her essay.

Imagine you have been asked to deliver the eulogy at Macbeth's funeral. Write the eulogy, incorporating as many of Lisa Low's arguments as you can.

by Stuart Dischell

Macbeth

Macbeth is vulnerable and all too human – because of his overly active imagination. This poem asks what made "the trees begin to move in?"

What in the sour wind
Made the voices come again
And the trees begin
To move in?

Spoken to
And spoken for,
You were waited upon
And waiting.

The leaves woke
On the windcombed branches,

And the footed trunks
Not in twos advanced
But like a lightless fire
From the hill descended.

*

You owned the motion
But you could not pray.

You owned the fortress
But you could not hide.

You owned the words
But they would not stay
The eight kings in your mind.

*

Hags in a circle dance
The nightmare day's full hours.
From their lips a pointed noise—
The cricket, the sword, the owl:

The assassin of the sleeping king
Stabbed by him cut from his mother's womb.
The soldiers lay down their broken boughs,
And the circle closes round him like a crown.

Write a poem or descriptive paragraph focussing on the power of Macbeth's imagination.

Write a poem expressing your thoughts and feelings about the character of Macbeth.

Paul Hewitt

Does Shakespeare deal with real life? Just how relevant is a study of a play like Macbeth *to the average person?*

Please, sir, I don't mean to be disrespectful.
I did raise my hand.
I mean, who cares if Macbeth becomes a monster,
If Huck Finn rescues Jim,
If Willie Loman never finds happiness?
They're just characters in books.
What have they got to do with me?
I mean, I'm never going hunting for white whales.
I'm never going to fight in the Civil War.
And I certainly don't live in the Dust Bowl.
Tell me instead how to
Make money, pick up girls.
Then maybe I'll listen.
You got any books that deal with real life?

Write a poem in response to Paul Hewitt's question. You may choose to agree or disagree with his position.

In groups, brainstorm all the possible reasons why Shakespeare would be considered important or relevant by our society today. You need not agree with all these reasons but offer them anyway.

Macbeth

by Liz Newall

Macbeth's smoldering ambition,
witch struck and lady
kindled.
left his ashen
conscience
floating daggers
in the smoke.

Do you agree with the view expressed in the limerick on page 30 and in Newall's poem that Lady Macbeth was responsible for the bloodshed that occurs in the play? Explain. You may wish to respond to this by writing a limerick or short poem.

Abstracts from Shakespeare

by Desmond Graham

In fact Macbeth
listened to his wife
then killed her
placed her in bed
beside dead Duncan
told the court
he caught them at it
killed them both:
thus he gained
the crown, a reputation
as a man of principle
and died, old,
in bed.

Write your own "abstract" on Macbeth in which you offer another alternative ending to the play.

William Shakespeare: Macbeth

by Mary Holtby

Read this poem carefully and see if anything of significance has been left out.

This is the life of Mac the Knife
whose fate was foretold by witches:
They said he'd be King, so he and his wife
worked out the possible hitches.
When good King Dunc in sleep was sunk,
they thrust him through with a dagger,
And although poor Mac was blue with
  funk
he carried it off with a swagger.
The King was dead, the princes fled,
and the kingdom Mac's for the taking,
But Banq's for the chop since the witches
  said
his sons were kings in the making.
The thugs are slow off the mark, and so
they half-complete their mission,
But enough to make Mac's party go
when he sees Banq's apparition;
This bloodstained ghost upsets the host
but makes him even keener
To put his enemies on toast,
and take them to the cleaner.
The witches bluff him with some stuff
which is truthful yet deceiving;
His target is now the tough Macduff,
who's off to England, leaving
His wife and chicks to cross the Styx,
fit tidings to incite him
To end the tyrant's testy tricks,
so he joins the prince to fight him.
Meanwhile the Knife observes his wife
parade, out-out-damn-spotting—
Curses the shadow-play of life,
such pointless parts allotting.
Now branches hood his foes—not good
for Mac, who, white as linen,
Recalls what's said of Birnam Wood
advancing to Dunsinane.
Still he won't run—no woman's son
slays this predestinarian...
Macduff explains he isn't one
(a posthumous Caesarian);
His sword goes smack through poor old
  Mac—
alas for realm and riches!
It's better to endure their lack
than put your trust in witches.

In groups of five, prepare a performance of this poem. Include a lively reading as well as action in your performance. Remember that it is not necessary to speed through the reading part.

AFFAIRS *of* DEATH

by Kingsley Amis

According to history, Macbeth was actually quite a good king and he had as much right to the throne as Duncan. In this short story based on historical fact, we see a Macbeth quite different from the portrait painted by Shakespeare.

Autumn had come early and the weather had turned bleak and damp. My delight at returning to Rome was tempered by apprehension about what might have been in store for me there. I need not have worried, however; Hildebrand the Benedictine had kept everything safe and I found the City perfectly quiet. I had sent ahead and he was waiting up for me in the yellow saloon, where a cold supper had been laid. He greeted me with a precise blend of reverence and warmth.

"Well, what awaits my attention tomorrow?" I asked.

"Many things, great and small. None pressing. One pleasant matter. There is a king in Rome, most eager for an audience with your highness. I think I never saw one more truly eager."

"What king?"

"Of Scots or Scotland, Macbeth by name. He has been here a week or more in hope. It might be entertaining."

"Entertaining or not, I will see him. Of course I will. I must make any friends I can. If he cares to call on me I will receive the king of Vinland. How is he attended, this Macbeth?"

"By nobody. By somebody I took for a kind of soldier. He was here, King Macbeth was in Rome, three years ago on purpose to see your highness, but you were abroad then, peregrinating beyond the Alps."

"Yes, yes. Such persistence merits reward. Arrange it."

"It is done, Lord. Provisionally. Noon, not tomorrow but the day following. Now your highness must retire," said Hildebrand, summoning servants. "And sleep late."

When, somewhat refreshed after twelve hours in a good bed, I rose the next afternoon, Hildebrand was soon in attendance again with information about Scotland. The country, or the territory inhabited by Scots, was confined to that part of the mainland of Britain which lies north of the Firth of Forth. Here and over neighbouring regions from the furthest shores of the Irish Sea to those of the North Sea, there ranged at different times bands of Irish, Picts, Scots, Britons, Angles, Cumbrians, English, Danes, Norwegians contending in prolonged and obscure struggles. That end of northern Europe had been a violent place for centuries and seemingly still was.

At first sight Scotland was no concern of mine. The Church was well enough established there, and Macbeth had shown himself well disposed to her. I had no way of controlling events. There was only one bishop of the Scots, at St. Andrews, and his influence was purely local. What monks there were had no power. Clearly, the key to control of the Scottish church lay in the sovereign. If I could win some personal regard from Macbeth, I might be laying the foundations of something that might, again, prove useful in any future trouble with England. And that there would be trouble with England, sooner or later, if not in my time then in that of one or other of my successors, I had not the slightest doubt.

I hardly know what I had expected to encounter the noon following, certainly not the tall, fair-haired, blue-eyed figure in his late forties who was presented; I thought he might well have had a Norse ancestor as well as Norse neighbours. His companion, introduced by my usher as Captain Seaton, short, broad, heavily bearded, with a look of stupid ferocity, was much more my idea of a Scotchman. As the two knelt before me I bestowed on each a salutation appropriate to his rank.

So as not to overawe my visitors excessively I had received them in a small throne-room built two centuries before by my predecessor Agapetus II and not two storeys high, none the less worthy of its function with sumptuous new frescoes, sculptures in the round and jewelled appointments. Here King Macbeth sat, sat sufficiently at his ease with his blue eyes reverentially lowered. Without much confidence in being understood, I asked in simple Latin a question about his earlier visit to the City.

Unexpectedly once more, he replied in fluent and correct French, my own native tongue, "I was desperately disappointed to be unable to pay my respects to your highness. I had to be content with distributing money to the poor of Rome."

"Do many of your countrymen share your majesty's remarkable skill?" I asked in the same language, already in some degree impressed.

"Alas no, Holy Father. I have been fortunately placed. It so happens that over the past two years I have sheltered at my court a number of French-speaking fugitives from England, and I sent myself to school with them. After all, this conversation, however memorable to me, would have been much restricted otherwise. My Latin is rudimentary, and I doubt if your highness's Gaelic is any better."

I laughed, partly in unconcealed appreciation of this speech. "Doubtless you made other visits on your journey here, your majesty?" I asked, deciding to probe a little.

He was on the defensive at once. "Yes, Holy Father, one such, but it was of no importance, not even comparatively so."

"Nevertheless, I trust enjoyable?"

"I must ask your highness to pardon me," he said, blinking fiercely.

This time I suppressed a smile. It was as clear to me as from a full description that what he had visited or attempted to visit was William's court, and no less so that he had been rebuffed—unseen, I judged, for it took no more than a glance to show that here was a man to be reckoned with, not the refined soul he took himself for, a barbarian still, but a remarkable barbarian. "We hear pleasing reports of the state of Scotland under your majesty's stewardship."

"Your highness is too kind. And you bring me to the object of this interview, or the secondary object, the first plainly being to be granted your blessing, Holy Father. I hope to be forgiven for making what must be an unusual request. It is that a clerk should be sent for to record the substance of what, if permitted, I shall say."

I gave the necessary directions, and simply waited, mastering my curiosity as best I could.

"I suppose you know little of Scotland, Holy Father. It is a remote and obscure place, its people wild, ignorant, credulous, superstitious, not brutish but childish. They have no notions of probability, of consistency, of what is real and what is fancied. My reign has not been untroubled and some of the events in it, and even more those attending its inception, were violent, confused and ambiguous. Not long after I am dead the generally accepted account of it, of my reign, is likely to deviate absurdly and irrecoverably from historical fact. A like process has already distorted the years of my predecessor's rule. With your help, Holy Father, I intend to set on record the truth of these matters and to leave that record lodged in the bosom of the see of St. Peter, where it will be safe for ever. What I have to say may also attract your highness's passing attention, for all Scotland's distance from the centre of the world."

This last stroke, and the glance that went with it, caused me to reflect that such men as this were not very common anywhere, not even in Rome. Just then a clerk appeared, a Benedictine, and on my nod settled himself at Macbeth's left side. I spread the palm of one hand in invitation.

"Some things are seen, some things are put out of sight. It is seen that old Malcolm II, King of Scots, fortunate, victorious, praised of bards, had no son to follow him, but that he ruled so long that by the time he died his grandsons were grown up. For the succession, it is seen that he favoured the eldest, Duncan. This, when he might have chosen the third in age, myself, or even the fourth and youngest, Thorfinn Sigurdson, son of the Norwegian earl of Orkney. By the ancient custom of our royal house the eldest prince has no firm right to succeed, and I had a better claim, a double claim, a claim not only through my own lineage but also through that of my wife Gruoch, granddaughter of King Kenneth III, whom old Malcolm had deposed and killed. Such a claim as hers is also admitted by our custom.

"All this is seen. It is further seen though ill remembered, that old Malcolm made over to Thorfinn, with the title of earl, two fiefs on the mainland, this as a means of placating any ambition he might nourish, of restraining him. The old man had not reckoned that, once on the throne, the foolhardy Duncan would try to recover those places by force of arms. Scotland ran with blood, much of it that of my own people, some of it my own blood; I carried a sword for my king as a commander of his armies. One morning thirteen years ago, Thorfinn's Norwegians burst upon the Scots from the rising sun at Burghead in Moray and cut them to pieces on the beach in ten minutes. Duncan fled, and I and a party of my followers fled with him. Moray was my fief; by secret paths I led him to an abandoned fort at a place called Bothnagowan. There, one August night, we seized our chance, a dozen of us, and surprised him as he lay asleep out on the rampart, and stabbed him to death with our daggers. With no delay I had myself proclaimed king and was crowned at Scone, made peace with my cousin Thorfinn, made him my friend; indeed, he had been my friend before, he who always does what he has said he will do. And the Scots hung up their arms.

"This too is seen by some. What is not seen, what is already forgotten, what is put out of sight is Duncan as he was. Comely I grant him, with a bright eye and a curved lip, very like my father-in-law, as my wife often noted; both men were descended from Malcolm I, dead these hundred years. However, in all else Duncan was a wretch, mean of spirit, vengeful, I think a little mad; no one was safe from his sudden rages. Wasteful and indolent. Unclean in his person—he stank under our knives, not only from fear. Not kingly. It is put out of sight that his nickname of the Gracious was a jest, a taunt.

"Now Scotland is safe and at peace. This has not been customary; so fierce and prolonged have been her inner conflicts that, of her last nine kings, only old Malcolm died in his bed. The future holds some hope. Having no issue I have taken as my son the fruit of my wife's first marriage, young Lulach, a strong honest boy of twenty-one. I mean him to succeed me. Duncan's sons, Malcolm Broadhead and Donald Bane, whom I generously spared, shelter in the household of Siward, the English earl of Northumberland, a cousin of their mother's. They show no signs of moving to unseat me, nor can they ever contrive it while my friend and ally Thorfinn lives. Let them try and welcome. I will defend my country to my last breath.

"That all this is true I, Macbeth, King of Scots, swear on my honour.

"There remains the heavy matter of the killing of Duncan. It was done not in malice, it was done for Scotland, not for my advancement, it was done as an execution, not as a wanton slaying, but it was murder. If I am to bear the blame..."

As he paused I spoke. "Of that you and I will speak in private, your majesty, at a later hour. I must consider your tale."

"Thank you, Holy Father. Thank you, too, for giving me the opportunity of having it set down."

"You justified your forecast that it would catch my attention."

Macbeth nodded slowly, his thoughts on old wrongs and enduring hazards. It was more than half to himself that he said, "Already they are telling one another that my gentle Gruoch had a hand in Duncan's death, when in truth she was in my castle at Dunkeld, over sixty miles away. If it were not for this record, who could guess what might be believed of me in centuries to come? That I took innocent lives, that I murdered my friend, murdered children, that I consorted with witches and saw visions, that I—how to put it?—supped full with horrors."

Here he turned briefly to his man Seaton, and in a strange language spoke what I took to be some words of courteous apology for subjecting him to so much incomprehensible talk. The fellow gave a grunt of oafish surprise and faltered out a few harsh, graceless syllables, staring vacantly as he did so. Poor, poor King Macbeth; if that was his chosen associate, what must his daily company at home have been like? I would forgive him his murder; indeed, to have confined oneself to a single such crime in a country like Scotland, assuming the impression I had formed of it to be evenly moderately fair, indicated laudable restraint.

There were, of course, other considerations, other than the obvious diplomatic ones. A man likes to show mercy whenever possible. Then, at our private audience early that evening Macbeth relieved me of what might have been an awkwardness by tactfully producing unasked a quantity of gold and suggesting that I should devote it to pious purposes of my own choosing. And, when all is said, one soldier is bound to feel a certain kinship with another. It was with a full heart that I pronounced him absolved and wished him a safe return.

The next morning Hildebrand came to me with Macbeth's story written out fair. "To my mind, Lord, a considerable person."

"More so than his position calls for. I hope for his sake he sits as securely as he appears to believe."

"Time will show."

"Time will show many things of greater moment than the devices of a Scottish freebooter, however engaging."

"Is your highness telling me that this is not to be put into the permanent archive?"

"We agreed to keep it as sparse as possible. Extract whatever is needed."

"As your highness pleases. I hope you feel your time with Macbeth was not wasted."

"It was most interesting, and we have his goodwill." ■

The historical Macbeth visited Rome twice. This story deals with his second trip there. Write a short story based on Macbeth's first trip to Rome. Don't hesitate to elaborate on the few details provided or to make up incidents that are consistent with the characterization presented in this story.

Imagine that Macbeth's statement to the Pope has been rediscovered. Write a newspaper account of the discovery. Be sure to deal with the differences between the record and Shakespeare's treatment of Macbeth.

by Norrie Epstein

The Curse of "The Scottish Play"

Do you believe in curses? Actors do and most are convinced that the play Macbeth *is cursed. So afraid are they of the curse that they cannot bring themselves to say the "M" word nor can they quote from the play regardless of circumstances. They are convinced that if they do, bad luck is sure to follow.*

Macbeth is an unholy riddle we still hesitate to name for the fear of retribution.

—Michael Pennington

Macbeth is to the theatrical world what King Tut's tomb is to archaeologists. No other play has had more bad luck associated with it: coronaries, car accidents, mysterious ailments, botched lines, and sword wounds. The theatrical superstition is not taken lightly: even to pronounce the play's title is considered bad dressing-room form. Its very name is a curse, and actors will use any euphemism rather than actually say the "M" word. It's also considered as the height of bad dressing-room form to quote from the play under any circumstances. For hundreds of years it's been delicately referred to as "The Scottish Play" or simply "*That* Play."

How did the superstition originate? Is it because of the sinister atmosphere that shrouds the play with its cackling Witches, shrieking night birds, and damp swirling fogs? Or perhaps it's because unpleasant events seem to occur whenever it is performed.

- During the play's very first performance, on August 7, 1606, Hal Berridge, the boy who played Lady Macbeth, died backstage.
- In 1849, after years of intense animosity, the rivalry between the American actor Edwin Forrest and the British actor John Macready culminated in a riot in which thirty-one people were killed. It took place in front of the theatre where Macready was appearing in *Macbeth*.
- In one memorable week at the Old Vic in 1934, the play went through four different Macbeths. Michael Kim came down with laryngitis; Alastair Sim caught a

chill; and Marius Goring was fired. John Laurie survived to finish the run.

- The 1937 Laurence Olivier—Judith Anderson production at the Old Vic must have been the unluckiest ever. Just before the scheduled opening night Lilian Baylis's favorite dog, Snoo, died. (Miss Baylis was the founder of the Old Vic.) The next day, Miss Baylis herself succumbed after learning that the opening night was to be postponed. According to Olivier's biographer, Donald Spoto, the director "barely escaped death in a taxi accident; Olivier was nearly brained by a falling stage sandbag; the scenery did not fit the stage; and [composer] Darius Milhaud was not happy with his musical score and kept tearing up pages of his composition." Moreover, Olivier, with characteristic gusto, accidentally wounded the various Macduffs in the final battle scene.
- The Scottish Play seems to have given Miss Baylis a particularly hard time: when *Macbeth* opened in 1954 her portrait fell off the wall and smashed into pieces.
- In 1938 the Stratford Festival opened with a production of *Macbeth.* During that season an old man had both his legs broken when he was hit by his own car in the parking lot; Lady Macbeth ran her car into a store window; and Macduff fell off his horse and had to be replaced by an understudy for several days.
- Not even animals are immune: in Orson Welles and John Houseman's all-black "Voodoo *Macbeth,*" five live black goats were sacrificed late one night by Abdul, a genuine witch doctor who was part of the cast.
- A warning to critics who pan Macbeth: After the first night's performance of "Voodoo *Macbeth,*" Percy Hammond, the conservative drama critic of the New York *Herald Tribune,* wrote a scathing review criticizing the New Deal and the government's endowment for the arts, calling the production "an exhibition of deluxe boondoggling." Shortly after the review appeared, John Houseman was visited by the group of African drummers who appeared in the play, along with Abdul. According to Houseman's account in his autobiography, *Unfinished Business,* they wanted to know if the review was evil and if it was the work of an enemy: "He is a bad man?" Houseman concurred: "A bad man."

The next day Welles and Houseman were greeted by the theatre manager with some unsettling news: the theatre's basement had been filled all night with "unusual drumming and with chants more weird and horrible than anything that had been heard upon the stage." Welles and Houseman "looked at each other for an instant, then quickly away again, for in the afternoon paper...was a brief item announcing the sudden illness of the well-known critic Percy Hammond...[who] died some days later—of pneumonia, it was said." ■

Write a short story or poem in which you bring to life one of the "accidents" mentioned by Epstein in this selection.

If you are interested in learning more about the curse of the "Scottish Play," here are two books that you can consult:

Clark, Cumberland: *Shakespeare and the Supernatural*
London: Williams and Norgate

Hugget, Richard: *The Curse of Macbeth and Other Theatrical Superstitions: An Investigation*
Clippenham: Picton, 1981

REVIEWERS

The publishers and editors would like to thank the following educators for contributing their valuable expertise during the development of the *Global Shakespeare Series*:

Nancy Alford
Sir John A. Macdonald High School
Hubley, Nova Scotia

Dr. Philip Allingham
Golden Secondary School
Golden, British Columbia

Carol Brown
Walter Murray Collegiate Institute
Saskatoon, Saskatchewan

Rod Brown
Wellington Secondary School
Nanaimo, British Columbia

Brian Dietrich
Queen Elizabeth Senior Secondary School
Surrey, British Columbia

Alison Douglas
McNally High School
Edmonton, Alberta

Kim Driscoll
Adam Scott Secondary School
Peterborough, Ontario

Burton Eikleberry
Grants Pass High School
Grants Pass, Oregon

Gloria Evans
Lakewood Junior Secondary School
Prince George, British Columbia

Professor Averil Gardner
Memorial University
St. John's, Newfoundland

Joyce L. Halsey
Lee's Summit North High School
Lee's Summit, Missouri

Carol Innazzo
St. Bernard's College
West Essendon, Victoria, Australia

Winston Jackson
Belmont Secondary School
Victoria, British Columbia

Marion Jenkins
Glenlyon-Norfolk School
Victoria, British Columbia

Dr. Sharon Johnston
Boone High School
Orlando, Florida

Jean Jonkers
William J. Dean Technical High School
Holyoke, Massachusetts

Beverly Joyce
Brockton High School
Brockton, Massachusetts

Judy Kayse
Huntsville High School
Huntsville, Texas

Doreen Kennedy
Vancouver Technical Secondary School
Burnaby, British Columbia

Ed Metcalfe
Fleetwood Park Secondary School
Surrey, British Columbia

Janine Modestow
William J. Dean Technical High School
Holyoke, Massachusetts

Steve Naylor
Salmon Arm Senior Secondary School
Salmon Arm, British Columbia

Kathleen Oakes
Implay City Senior High School
Romeo, Michigan

Carla O'Brien
Lakewood Junior Secondary School
Prince George, British Columbia

Bruce L. Pagni
Waukegan High School
Waukegan, Illinois

Larry Peters
Lisgar Collegiate
Ottawa, Ontario

Margaret Poetschke
Lisgar Collegiate
Ottawa, Ontario

Jeff Purse
Walter Murray Collegiate Institute
Saskatoon, Saskatchewan

Grant Shaw
Elmwood High School
Winnipeg, Manitoba

Debarah Shoultz
Columbus North High School
Columbus, Indiana

Tim Turner
Kiona-Benton High School
Benton City, Washington

James Walsh
Vernon Township High School
Vernon, New Jersey

Kimberly Weisner
Merritt Island High School
Merritt Island, Florida

Ted Wholey
Sir John A. Macdonald High School
Hubley, Nova Scotia

Beverley Winny
Adam Scott Secondary School
Peterborough, Ontario

About the Series Editors

Dom Saliani, Senior Editor of the *Global Shakespeare Series*, is the Curriculum Leader of English at Sir Winston Churchill High School in Calgary, Alberta. He has been an English teacher for over 25 years and has published a number of poetry and literature anthologies.

Chris Ferguson is currently employed as a Special Trainer by the Southwest Educational Development Laboratory in Austin, Texas. Formerly the Department Head of English at Burnet High School in Burnet, Texas, she has taught English, drama, and speech communications for over 15 years.

Dr. Tim Scott is an English teacher at Melbourne Grammar School in Victoria, Australia, where he directs a Shakespeare production every year. He wrote his Ph.D. thesis on Elizabethan drama.

ACKNOWLEDGEMENTS

Permission to reprint copyrighted material is gratefully acknowledged. Every reasonable effort has been made to contact copyright holders. Any information that enables the publisher to rectify any error or omission will be welcomed.

Macbeth and the Witches by Richard Armour. Copyright © 1957 by Richard Armour. Reprinted by permission of John Hawkins & Associates, Inc. *The Imagery of Macbeth* by Caroline Spurgeon from SHAKESPEARE'S IMAGERY. Reprinted with permission of Cambridge University Press. *When Was the Murder of Duncan First Plotted?* by A.C. Bradley from SHAKESPEAREAN TRAGEDY: LECTURES ON HAMLET, OTHELLO, KING LEAR, MACBETH by A.C. Bradley. Reproduced with permission of Macmillan Press. *On the Knocking at the Gate in Macbeth* by Thomas De Quincey from MACBETH: CRITICAL ESSAYS by Samuel Schoenbaum. Reprinted with permission of Marilyn Schoenbaum for Samuel Schoenbaum. *The Macbeth Murder Mystery* by James Thurber. Copyright © 1942 James Thurber. Copyright © 1970 Rosemary Thurber. From MY WORLD - AND WELCOME TO IT, published by Harcourt Brace. *Macbeth as the Third Murderer* by Harold C. Goddard from THE MEANING OF SHAKESPEARE. Chicago: University of Chicago, 1951, pp. 107-35. Reprinted with permission of University of Chicago Press. *James I* by Rudyard Kipling from RUDYARD KIPLING'S COMPLETE VERSE by Rudyard Kipling. A.P. Watt Limited. *A Scene Left Out of Shakespeare's Macbeth* by William Davenant from Davenant's Macbeth from the YALE MANUSCRIPT: An Edition, with a Discussion of the Relation of Davenant's Text to Shakespeare's by Christopher Spencer. Yale University Press, 1961. Reprinted with permission. *"Out, Out..."* by Robert Frost from THE POETRY OF ROBERT FROST edited by Edward Connery Latham. Copyright by Robert Frost 1944. Copyright 1916 by Henry Holt and Co., Inc. © 1969 by Henry Holt and Co., Inc. Reprinted by permission of Henry Holt and Co., Inc. Henry Holt and Company. *At the Fire and Cauldron Health-Food Restaurant* by Martin Robbins. First published in the Sewanee Review, vol. 101, no. 4, Fall 1993. Copyright 1993 by Martin Robbins. Reprinted with permission of the editor and the author's agent. *Three Tragic Themes* by Edith Sitwell from MACBETH. First published in the Atlantic Monthly. *Ridding Ourselves of Macbeth* by Lisa Low. Reprinted from the Massachusetts Review, © 1984, The Massachusetts Review, Inc. *Macbeth* by Stuart Dischell. Stuart Dischell is the author of "Good Hope Road," a national poetry series selection and "Evenings and Avenues," both available from Penguin Books. *Paul Hewitt* from CLASS DISMISSED II by Mel Glenn. Text copyright © 1986 by Mel Glenn. Reprinted by permission of Clarion Books/Houghton Mifflin Company. All rights reserved. *Macbeth* by Liz Newall. Reprinted with permission of THE SHAKESPEARE NEWSLETTER, edited by Louis Marden. *Abstracts from Shakespeare* by Desmond Graham from ENGLISH volume 39, number 164, Summer 1990. Copyright The English Association 1990. Reprinted by permission of the publisher. *William Shakespeare: Macbeth* by Mary Holtby from HOW TO BECOME RIDICULOUSLY WELL READ IN ONE EVENING. *Affairs of Death* by Kingsley Amis from SHAKESPEARE STORIES by Giles Gordon. *The Curse of The Scottish Play* by Norrie Epstein from THE FRIENDLY SHAKESPEARE by Norrie Epstein.

ARTWORK

Yuan Lee: cover, 10, 16-17, 31, 34, 42-43, 49, 52, 64-65, 72, 74, 91, 92, 100-101, 110, 112, 113; **IGNITION Design and Communications**: series logo; marginal art: 15, 26, 36, 44, 48, 59, 62, 77, 96, 105; **John James**: 7, from *Shakespeare's Theatre* (Simon and Schuster, 1994); **Tom Taylor**: 8; **Nicholas Vitacco**: 9; flower and serpent from *A Choice of Emblemes*, reprinted by permission of the Folger Shakespeare Library: 25; "Lady Macbeth and the Sleeping Duncan" by William Blake from the Koriyama City Museum of Art: 40; soldiers' camp from *Holinshed's Chronicles*, 1577. Reprinted by permission of the Folger Shakespeare Library: 89; **Sharif Tarabay**: 78-79; bear-baiting from Charles Knight's *Pictorial Edition of the Works of Shakspere*, 1839-1843: 105; painting of James I from the Mary Evans Picture Library: 139; **Marc Mongeau**: 115, 118, 120; **Thom Sevalrud**: 122; **Don Tate**: 134; **Pierre-Paul Pariseau**: 141; **Harvey Chan**: 143; **Russ Wilms**: 144; **Leon Zernitsky**: 149; **Tracey Wood**: 156.